RHODODENDRONS

WITH
CAMELLIAS and MAGNOLIAS
1998

Published in 1998 by
The Royal Horticultural Society,
80 Vincent Square, London SW1P 2PE

ISBN 1 874431 62 0

Edited for the RHS by Karen Wilson

Honorary Editor for the Rhododendron, Camellia and Magnolia Group
Philip Evans

Editorial Subcommittee
Maurice Foster
Rosemary Foster
Brian Wright

Printed by Friary Press, Dorset

Contents

Foreword

John Bond

I have acquired a number of tasks on taking up my new role as Chairman of the Rhododendron, Camellia and Magnolia Group but none that I count as great a privilege as writing the Foreword for the Year Book. As I write these notes in my study I can see clearly not only the complete run of the Year Book from 1946 to date but also complete sets of the Notes of the Rhododendron Society and the Year Books of the Rhododendron Association. All of these offer a great wealth of valuable information; in fact, it is dangerously time-consuming to look at any one of the volumes for there is so much to occupy the reader for hours.

Readers will, I hope, realise when reading these notes why I count the opportunity to write this foreword a privilege. As any new Chairman on taking office should, I have taken stock of the Group's various activities and I have placed the Year Book at the top of the list. It holds this position in view of its value in holding the Group together, for it is, together with *The Bulletin*, the important link with the Executive Committee and the membership. It also belongs at the top for its interesting and valuable content, and this volume is no exception.

The excitement of rhododendrons in the wild is covered in Stephen Fox's mouth-watering A Forest of *lanatoides* and Keith Rushforth's paper Further Rhododendron Hunting in Vietnam, while hybrids are viewed from across the atlantic in Harold Greer's Pick of the US Hybrids.

The paper on the Ghent deciduous azalea hybrids will provide me, and I am sure many others, with much information of value. I am personally very fond of these small flowered hybrids which add considerable charm to our gardens.

Camellias are not forgotten. Two papers on the lovely *Camellia sasanqua* form will whet our appetites for these lovely shrubs, while Vonnie Cave describes some of the very fine camellias that have been raised in New Zealand.

Peter Borlase flies the magnolia flag high with a paper on his three stars. Maurice Foster brings us down to earth when he writes on magnolias from seed and, lastly, Robin Herbert outlines the experiences of the Magnolia Society when, as I understand, the party positively wallowed in magnolias at the Chollipo Arboretum, Korea.

Finally, I would like to welcome our new Editor, Philip Evans, and thank him for all the hard work he has applied to this Year Book. Bruce Archibold, my predecessor, expressed appreciation last year on behalf of us all to Cynthia Postan who retired as Editor last year. I, for my part, would like to thank Bruce Archibold for all the hard work, expertise and time he has given the Group which has provided me with such a smooth handover.

EDITORIAL

PHILIP EVANS

In taking on the Editorship for the Group, of the Year Book, I am conscious of inheriting responsibility for a publication whose present quality and popularity owes a very great deal to the work and dedication of Cynthia Postan, my predecessor. I hope that this, the first issue that I have compiled, is evidence of my intention to do my best to maintain the standard she has set, and to provide content that offers both variety and an interesting coverage of all three genera.

Variety must also mean diversity of authorship and I am pleased that we have contributors not only from the British Isles but also from Australia, Belgium, New Zealand, Switzerland and the USA.

Even a superficial study of the range of subject matter that has arisen in the Group's Year Books since 1946 (not a bad preparation for Editorship), leaves one with an overwhelming sense of the treasurehouse of knowledge they constitute in their entirety. The task undertaken by Stephen Fox at the request of the Executive Committee – the creation of a computer based Composite Year Book Index (and about which he has written a short article) – is very timely. Hopefully, when arrangements for its sale and distribution have been completed, it will help make this legacy of information more easily accessible to both our membership and to other students of the genera.

PICK OF THE NORTH AMERICAN HYBRIDS

HAROLD GREER

The assignment, discuss American hybrids. I thought that should be easy, but wait a minute, where do I begin and where do I end? What do I include and what do I leave out? There are so many North American hybrids and hybridizers.

First and foremost, we should look at the hybrids that have been awarded the highest and most prestigious award that the American Rhododendron Society offers, the Superior Plant Award, known as the SPA. In the more than 30 years this award has been available, it has been awarded only seven times. The award was first given in 1971 and two rhododendrons, 'Trude Webster' SPA and 'Lem's Cameo' SPA were the receivers. It was then 11 years before it was awarded again to 'Party Pink' SPA in 1983, to 'Ginny Gee' SPA and 'Patty Bee' SPA in 1985, to 'Taurus' SPA in 1990, followed by 'Scintillation' in 1991, the last time this award was given. All of these plants are outstanding in their own way. 'Trude Webster' is a huge and perfect pink that shines at its best on a cool spring day. 'Lem's Cameo' with its luscious peachy flowers has been extensively used in many newer hybrids. Both do best in the northwest part of North America. 'Party Pink' and 'Scintillation' which are both pinks were developed in the eastern part of

the US where temperatures are colder, therefore they have much greater cold hardiness. 'Taurus', the only red in the group, an outstanding plant for both foliage and flower was also developed in the northwest. 'Ginny Gee' which is pink to white, and 'Patty Bee' which is yellow, are both small leaved lepidote hybrids that are very compact and low growing. All of these SPA plants should be excellent in the British Isles.

An area of special interest, has been the introduction of yellow and orange rhododendrons. The deepest yellow would still be 'Hotei', though 'Odee Wright', a lighter yellow is easier to grow. Other significant yellows would be 'Nancy Evans', a hybrid of 'Hotei' × 'Lem's Cameo', 'Top Banana', 'Morning Sunshine', 'Sunspray', 'Gold Medal' and the giant flowered 'Horizon Monarch' a hybrid of 'Nancy Evans' × 'Point Defiance'. For orange-yellow bicolors, 'Ring of Fire', 'Flaming Star' and 'Nasalle' would have to head the list for their magnificent yellow-orange centre, edged by luscious hot orange. In orange rhododendrons, 'September Song' is a sure winner with its deep orange flowers. Then comes 'Whitney Orange', 'Old Copper' and 'Autumn Gold', the latter two have been around for nearly 40 years, but they are still more hardy and adaptable than many of the newer hybrids. There are many hybrids of 'Lem's Cameo' now being developed that promise to be very good. As a general rule, most yellow and orange rhododendrons are best suited to areas with relatively mild winters and cool summers and were developed in western North America. More yellow and orange hybrids are being developed in the colder winter and hotter summer areas of eastern North America, and some good hybrids are beginning to appear, though there is much work yet to be done.

Red hybrids of exceptional beauty are often hybrids of the Dutch hybrid 'The Honorable Jean Marie de Montague'. 'Halfdan Lem', 'Markeeta's Prize', 'Britton Hill', and the more rose coloured 'Hallelujah' are excellent examples and are plants of exceptional merit. The Honorable Jean Marie de Montague hybrids tend not to be rock hardy and are best as northwest hybrids or hybrids for the British Isles. Contrast this with the *R. catawbiense* hybrids such as 'Henry's Red' which while a nice red, is not as showy as those that can be grown in a more temperate climate. Two other reds of special note for their almost 'black' colour are 'Black Magic' (another 'The Honorable Jean Marie de Montague' hybrid) and 'Martian King'.

For pink to rose, we have already mentioned some, though any article on American hybrids would be remiss not to mention 'Lem's Monarch' (also known as 'Pink Walloper'), 'Point Defiance', 'Anna Rose Whitney', 'Very Berry' and 'Hallelujah' with its interesting deep green, down turned leaves. This plant should be grown if only for its foliage. However, if you live in an area of high winds, give it wind protection.

In blue and purple elepidote hybrids, it is hard to chose as there are many. 'Blue Jay', while not a collector's dream, has become an excellent plant for the landscape. It flowers late and is very rugged. Other darker blues or blue-purples include 'Blue Lagoon', 'Peter Allan', 'Dorothy Amateis' and the very cold hardy deep purple 'Jonathan Shaw'. Outstanding for its waxy red-purple perfect shaped trusses is 'Olin O. Dobbs'. It wins top prizes in rhododendron shows, and watching the list of winners from rhododendron shows, it often is at the top of the list. A hybrid worth mentioning for its late flowering is 'Plum Beautiful' with medium purple flowers with a black purple flare.

The choice of white hybrids is much shorter and I feel too few people try to hybridize for excellent white rhododendrons. 'Pawhuska', 'Travis L', 'Dolly Madison' and 'Wynterset White' come to mind, though there are others, especially *R. yakushimanum* hybrids which often start pink and turn white such as 'Yaku Princess' or 'Senator Henry Jackson'. 'Winter Snow' is also worth mentioning, as it is one of the few hybrids of *R. aberconwayi*. It is a compact growing plant with upright facing snow white flowers in compact trusses.

Like other hybridizers throughout the world, North American hybridizers are infatuated with producing hybrids of *R. yakushimanum* and an entire article could be written about them. Certainly for foliage they produce a superb group of plants, and three of the best are 'Cinnamon Bear', 'Teddy Bear' (both *R. bureavii* × *R. yakushimanum*), and 'Golfer' (*R. yakushimanum* × *R. pseudochrysanthum*). For excellent flowers, 'Centennial Celebration' which was named in honour of the State of Washington's 100th birthday is one to remember. A hybrid with 'Purple Lace', it has ruffled light orchid flowers. A hard plant to beat for both foliage and flowers is 'Noyo Brave'. It is a hybrid with 'Noyo Chief' which is known for its exceptional foliage. 'Noyo Brave' starts with deep rose-red buds, which open deep pink gradually changing to light pink and then almost white, giving the plant a candy stripe appearance. Along this same multiple colour appearance, comes 'Aloha' with its apricot pink flowers which lighten as the flowers age. There are few true red *R. yakushimanum* hybrids, but 'Skookum' and its sister 'Skookumchuck' are excellent second generation hybrids that maintain deep red coloration.

Much emphasis has been made by eastern North American hybridizers to produce very cold hardy and heat tolerant rhododendrons. Rhododendrons like 'Scintillation', 'Janet Blair', 'Casanova', 'Henry's Red' and of course many lepidotes such as the 'PJM' group fit this description.

Last, but not least, are the lepidote hybrids which have been produced in abundance. The 'PJM' group is certainly the leader in this group, but others such as 'Weston's Pink Diamond', 'Hudson Bay', 'Manitau' and 'Dora Amateis' are excellent hybrids containing the native eastern North American species *R. minus* var. *minus* Carolineanum Group. Two other species groups

used extensively are those from the subsect. Triflora and Lapponica. Examples here of excellent plants are 'Senora Meldon', 'Blaney's Blue', 'Mother Greer' and 'Mary Fleming'. There are also many wonderful very dwarf lepidotes such as 'Ginny Gee' and 'Patty Bee' which have already been mentioned. Others such as 'Wee Bee', 'Too Bee' and 'Honsu's Baby' deserve attention. The last group of lepidote hybrids are from Subsect. Maddenia and are probably hardy only in Cornwall and other warmer areas. 'Mi Amour' is certainly worthy and even received an Award of Merit from the RHS in 1975. 'My Lady' and 'Else Frye' are other plants worthy of attention.

I have not mentioned hybridizers names in this article, rather emphasising hybrids that should do well in the British Isles and not who produced them.

All in all, North America has for the past few years taken over the hybridizing that was once done by the big British estates, but hybridizing is open world-wide to growers of rhododendrons, and I am thankful that with rhododendrons there are no country boundaries, only people throughout the world that love rhododendrons!

HAROLD GREER *is the owner of Greer Gardens in Oregon USA and is the joint author of* Rhododendron Hybrids, *a standard work on the subject*

RHODODENDRONS FOR GREENHOUSES AND CONSERVATORIES

KENNETH & PETER COX

Growing rhododendrons indoors in conservatories and greenhouses seems to be something which periodically goes in and out of fashion. In Victorian times, Vireyas were very popular and many spectacular hybrids were created, many of which are now lost. Many of the great indoor rhododendron collections are no longer; the one at the Royal Botanic Garden, Edinburgh is much lamented in H H Davidian's *Rhododendron Species*. Several new collections of Maddenia and Edgeworthia species and hybrids have been started in recent years; among these are those at Glasnevin in Dublin, St Andrews Botanic Garden and at the Savill Gardens, Windsor Great Park, in an impressive new greenhouse with sides which open up completely. Perhaps some of these public collections will inspire others to make collections. Vireyas too are making a comeback with several UK nurseries now supplying them. This article concentrates on Maddenia species and their relatives.

To grow Maddenia subsect. and related rhododendrons indoors, you almost certainly need a greenhouse or conservatory: they are very seldom successful as houseplants as they need cool winter tempera-

tures; they should be kept just frost free, i.e. at a temperature too cold for normal human comfort. The dry air and low light levels combined with the high temperatures of a typical house in winter is definitely not conducive to rhododendron culture indoors. Ideally the individual plants if pot-grown can be brought from the greenhouse or conservatory into the house while they are in flower and returned when they are over. If there is room in the greenhouse to grow several, these can be selected so that they open their flowers in succession over several months and one or more can be brought into the house at a time. Many people put their pot-grown tender species and hybrids outside in a sheltered spot in summer to protect them from high summer temperatures in the glasshouse and to cut down on watering. If you do this, avoid too much shade or you won't get many flower buds set. Pot growing is not the only option. Many people grow indoor rhododendron in beds. Compost needs to be well drained, without too much peat but instead use coarse bark, needles, grit, perlite and similar materials. Drainage is improved if the beds are raised up from the level of the floor.

In areas of alkaline soil, the easiest way to grow rhododendrons is often in containers. This of course includes tender ones for inside. Collect rainwater and use this for watering as much as possible. An occasional soaking with alkaline water is unlikely to do any harm. Hardy rhododendrons can also be grown in containers and brought into the house when in flower.

You certainly don't need masses of space to grow Maddenia rhododendrons in a greenhouse. Even the more vigorous species and hybrids can be kept within bounds by pruning and they can grow close together, even somewhat tangled up in one another.

HYBRIDS
Scented

In growing the Maddenia species and hybrids, the feature most people want is scent; a single relatively small plant can perfume a large area when brought into the house in flower. Of the hybrids, the old favourite 'Fragrantissimum' is one of the most popular. Strongly-scented white flowers but uncontrollably straggly and untidy, it needs to be supported on a framework or trained to keep it in bounds. 'Lady Alice Fitzwilliam' has a scent almost as good but is much tidier in habit, making a neat, fairly compact plant. We have remade this cross using forms of the parents *R. ciliatum* and *R. edgeworthii* (see fig. 1) and the resulting scented selections make good plants in pots indoors or outside in the garden. A plant we received from Jim Russell as *R ciliicalyx* but which is undoubtedly a hybrid is perhaps the most spectacular of all the Maddenia hybrids we have seen. It has huge very frilly, scented white flowers with pale pink and yellow markings on a rangy but upright plant which can get to 1.8-2.4m (6-8ft) or more. For want of a proper name, we have distributed this as '*R. ciliicalyx* hybrid'. There are various other scented hybrids with names such as 'Else Frye' and 'Princess Alice' which are occasionally available from specialist nurseries.

Non-scented

There are many fine hybrids which have little or no scent. 'My Lady' is one of the finest of all in flower with large, pure white, perfectly formed trusses and a tidy habit. Other relatively tidy growers include 'Countess of Haddington', with rose-flushed flowers, and early flowerers with *R. moupinense* in the parentage such as the pink 'Jabberwocky' and our own white and pink *R. edgeworthii* × *R. moupinense*. Other neat growers include some of the yellow-flowered hybrids derived from species in both Subsects. Maddenia and Boothia such as *R. valentinianum*. Some of the best are the curious 'Moth' with long-lasting, thickly textured red spotted yellow flowers and a plant which is widely grown outdoors in western Scotland as *R. burmanicum* but which is actually a hybrid. Yellow-flowered species and hybrids have little or no scent. There are many new hybrids being raised in California, New Zealand and elsewhere which should add to the available range.

SPECIES

Many species are variable in the amount of scent they have, depending on the clone; within one species, scent can range from almost none to very strong. Most scented species have white flowers, often with a yellow blotch, while some are tinged pink. Those with the strongest scent include some forms of *R. edgeworthii* (but not the FCC form) and *R. formosum* var. *inaequale* and *R. coxianum*. Some *R. veitchianum* and *R. formosum* var. *formosum* also have a fine scent. Two lesser known species which are sometimes scented are the *R. scopulorum* from S E Tibet and *R dendricola*. *R. walongense* aff. C&H 373 is early flowering with a spicy scent and a beautiful deep mahogany-coloured bark. Some of the most strongly scented species such as *R. nuttallii* and *R. taggianum* are a bit on the large side for pot growing but are possible if you have enough space. Species such as *R. lindleyi* have such rangy straggly habits that they seldom look good in pots. Rather tidier in its growth are *R. megacalyx* and the newly introduced *R liliiflorum* (see fig. 2) which is one of the latest flowering species, usually into June.

Some species are well worth growing despite having little or no scent. *R. dalhousiae* var. *dalhousiae* is a vigorous grower with creamy flowers, often tinged yellow and/or green when first open, while var. *rhabdotum* has eye-catching red or deep pink stripes down each corolla lobe and is useful for its late flowering in June-July. Although most species are white or yellow, some selected forms have relatively pink flowers. Examples include *R. lindleyi* 'Geordie Sherriff' and certain selections of *R. edgeworthii*. A few species such as *R. carneum* and R. *horlickianum* are pale pink outdoors but tend to be near white indoors. Two yellow-flowered tender species are the rare *R. edgeworthii* relative *R. seinghkuense* with smaller leaves and flowers than its cousin and the bright yellow *R. chrysodoron*.

There is considerable confusion in the naming of both species and hybrids among the Maddenia and their relatives. In the case of the species, this is largely due to the considerable reduction of the number of species in Cullen's revision and his extensive renaming of specimens. For example, many plants formerly labelled *R. supranubium*, and *R. ciliicalyx* have now been placed in synonymy with or have been re-allocated to *R. pachypodum* and so plants are often circulating under two names. In addition, frankly there are still far too many virtually identical so-called species recognized; species such as *R. ciliicalyx*, *R. roseatum*, *R. ludwigianum*, *R. pachypodum*, *R. horlickianum* and *R. carneum* are so similar that really only known clones can be separated. The naming of hybrids is also very inconsistent. In comparing collections at Windsor, Mt Congreave and elsewhere it is obvious that many nurseries are distributing wrongly labelled Maddenia species and hybrids and that in the case of some such as 'Princess Alice' and 'Fragrantissimum' there appears to be more than one 'clone' in circulation. It would be useful to have a national collection set up with a view to systematically sorting out the confusion.

CULTIVATION: the keys to success:
1. Drainage. All appreciate good drainage. Many of the species are epiphytic in the wild, while those which are not are usually found on rocks and cliffs. The compost must be coarse with plenty of air spaces in it so water can run through easily. Coarse bark, perlite, woodchips, needles and grit are all possible ingredients. Avoid more than a small percentage of peat as it tends to hold

too much moisture, is usually too fine and eventually rots down into sludge.

2. Containers. If growing in pots, do not over pot; they like to have their roots restricted and over-potting can kill plants. Most do not mind being a bit pot-bound, though this means watering must be frequent in the growing season. Many people insist on earthenware pots as they absorb moisture and help good drainage. Unfortunately they also make the plants heavier! In fact plastic pots are fine if you keep a close eye on watering, but if the watering is to be left in someone else's hands for long spells, it might be advisable to use either earthenware pots or plastic ones with extra holes made in the sides. Another alternative is to use mesh pots of the type available for pond plants but there is a very limited range of sizes available and these need more frequent watering than any of the above.

3. Watering. Never water a pot that is already wet. Allow it to partially dry out before watering again. This is doubly necessary with those species that are usually epiphytic in nature such as *R. edgeworthii* and *R. seinghkuense*. Always test the weight of a pot by lifting it if you are not sure how wet it is. If allowed to dry out completely, it may be necessary to soak the pot in a basin or trough until thoroughly wet and then left to become slightly dry again before re-watering. In summer, in sunny weather, water every second day. In winter, every week or two may be enough. Avoid watering overhead as much as possible, except in sunny weather in summer, and always avoid watering overhead anything that is in flower as this tends to encourage either botrytis or petal blight (when the flowers rapidly turn to mush and stick on to the leaves below).

4. Beds. The same guidelines for containers apply to beds. Quick drainage through an open compost is desirable. The main disadvantage with beds is that the plants of course cannot be moved about. We have seen a few smallish greenhouses devoted to these tender rhododendrons that have become so overgrown that it is almost impossible to get inside the door, let alone admire the plants! Slower-growing species and hybrids are liable to get completely suppressed by those more vigorous. Most can be cut right back but after doing this once or twice, it is better to start again with small plants and completely renew the soil. Most are easy to root from cuttings.

5. Light and Air. Keep the growing area as cool and bright as possible in winter to discourage the flower buds falling off and to prevent the spread of disease. In summer, try to maintain some humidity. Very dry air can cause foliage browning or defoliation and bud abortion.

6. Pests and Diseases. Beware of vine weevil, mildew and rust. The former is the worst pest as currently there is so little effective action that can be taken against it by amateurs. The small white grubs are laid by the adults in summer and the larvae eat the roots or girdle the stem, often causing death. Professional growers use the chemicals chlorpyrifos and fonofos as a drench or better as a slow release granule which can be added to the compost and which lasts for up to two years. These may come on to the market for amateurs. Currently nematodes are the only recourse for the amateur. These are obtained by mail order and require a warm temperature to work effectively (this varies according to the type used). They are applied in a water solution and it is important to ensure that the nematodes penetrate well into the rootball. Apply from July onwards. Several of the hybrids including 'Fragrantissimum' and 'Lady Alice Fitzwilliam' are prone to powdery mildew and rust. Bupirimate with triforine (Nimrod 'T') and myclobutanil (Systhane) control both diseases. Mancozeb is good against rusts while propiconazole (Tumbleblight) is effective against mildew. Start spraying when new growth has developed and repeat every month or six weeks until growth stops in autumn. Other likely pests are aphids on young shoots, caterpillars and slugs eating young leaves, the latter especially on small plants.

7. Pruning. Pinch out single growth buds to encourage branching and/or prune hard after flowering, especially with straggly, aging plants. Most species and hybrids tend towards straggliness and if you don't prune, will soon become sparse, top heavy and of very little ornamental value. Don't leave pruning too late as you won't get flower buds the following year.

8. Feeding. Slow release fertilizer is very effective, but don't over do it. It can be incorporated into the compost when repotting or it is available in clusters to be pushed into the soil once a year around or just after flowering. Alternatively liquid feed or granular feed can be applied. Don't apply much after June if you want a good bud set in the following year.

9. Repotting. This should be done annually for the first few seasons while a plant is growing rapidly, but then onwards, repotting every two to three years is perfectly adequate

if regularly fed and good health is maintained. Increase pot size gradually. Make sure that the root ball is thoroughly wet through and that the edges of the new pot are full of compost without ramming it in hard. Leave 2-3cm (¾-1¼in)depth space at the top of the pot to hold plenty of water when watering. When the containers get large and further repotting becomes undesirable or impossible, knock out the root ball, scratch out some old compost top and bottom and replace with some fresh compost. This treatment should keep plants going for many years and may also be done for younger plants in years between repotting.

10. Regular maintenance. Go over all pots at least twice a year, checking to see that the pot is adequately full of compost, removing any dead leaves, weeds and liverwort. Moss is a natural ground cover in the wild and a thin moss cover is perfectly acceptable. The development of liverwort is often a sign of overpotting. The soil becomes easily overwet and death of the plant may result. Remove yellowing leaves, dead branches and dead heads in season. Plants in beds should be treated likewise and benefit from an annual mulch of leafmould, rotted bracken, bark, conifer needles or chipped conifer tops. Like most rhododendrons, if cherished and loved, these tender ones should live for many years and may even outlive us and be passed on to the next generation.

PETER AND KENNETH COX, *of Glendoick Gardens Ltd, Perth, father and son, are the joint authors of several well known books about rhododendrons, including their latest reviewed in this* Year Book

Stephen Fox

In Year Book No. 45 (1993), page 32, I gave an account of the discovery of *Rhododendron lanatoides* by Kingdon-Ward in 1924 and of the strange circumstances which led to a few descendent plants being cultivated in Britain for more than 50 years before they were recognized as belonging to a new species.

In the wild, the known locations of *R. lanatoides* are all in south-east Tibet and within a dozen miles of one another. Until recently only three collections had been made: south of the Tsangpo on the Nam La and on the Taku Pu La, and north of the Rong Chu on the Sobhe La. In none of these places was the plant reported to have colonized.

When south-east Tibet was re-opened to tourists in 1995, it was hoped to rediscover *R. lanatoides*, but in that we were disappointed. (See Year Book No. 48 [1996-97], page 18.) However, while leading the 1996 Exodus group, Kenneth Cox sighted a single plant of the elusive species on the Serge La (between Ningshi and Tumbatse). Later, on the Tra La, east of Lunang, he found 'a forest' of it.

I decided to see for myself and joined the 1997 Exodus party. Apparently the Serge La plant had disappeared in a landslide but as we ascended the Tra La, at around 3,800m (12,500ft), a few plants of *R. lana-toides* began to appear among the usual rhododendron flora of *R. wardii*, *R. vellereum* (*principis*) and *R. uvarifolium*. At about 4,100m (13,450ft), still within the rhododendron forest, the path ran parallel to the northern rim of a steep-sided gully, and as I looked down I was amazed to see that it did indeed contain a forest of *R. lanatoides* and little other vegetation. The gully, perhaps 50m (164ft) wide, sloped down to the west and the *R. lanatoides* grew over a vertical range of about 300m (985ft). The plants grew to a height of about 7m (23ft) and in mid-June the flowers were mostly over. However one specimen on the rim had been knocked or blown over to a near-horizontal position and it was still in bloom (see fig. 6). Nearby, there grew a few plants which were evidently natural hybrids with the neighbouring species. In the rain it was a gloomy scene as the forest was dense, the cloud dark and the mist thick. The forest litter was covered with luxuriant moss, confirming that the wetness we were experiencing was nothing unusual.

This discovery removes any lingering doubts regarding the status of this striking foliage plant as a species.

We found no *R. lanatoides* on the Temo La, nor on the Nyima La but another rhododendron enthusiast whom we met reported sightings on the Tang La and at other locations within the Rong Chu watershed, mostly on west-facing slopes at around 4,000m (13,125ft).

R. *lanatoides* in cultivation

In 1992 I was optimistic that *R. lanatoides* would soon become generally available in the nursery trade. Unfortunately this has not happened. No truly compatible rootstock for grafts has been found, so many grafted plants have snapped off while others have developed swellings at the union, or have died without obvious cause. Rooting seems impossible. Self-pollinated seed from the plants in cultivation has proved infertile or has bred short-lived weaklings. Cross-polli-

nation between the clones in cultivation has not been attempted on account of their geographical separation and their different times of flowering.

New clones from wild-collected seed are now being established and a few will be offered for sale. I doubt if they will be quick to flower: when they do, cross-pollination will provide the means of propagating the species in quantity – and doubtless of hybridizing with other foliage plants.

STEPHEN FOX *is a member of the Group, resident in the Peak District, and a keen student of the origins and cultivation of rhododendrons*

Towards the Doker La
The BNNZ Expedition to Yunnan

DAVID FARNES

Following my first trip to China in 1994 with the expedition led by Ted Millais, I was invited by The Sichuan Service Corporation for Scientific Expeditions to bring my own expedition to China, but I could not contemplate such a venture until the spring of 1997.

In the event the planned itinerary became a hybrid between the more popular tourist-explorer trail from Kunming to Dequen via Dali, Lijiang and Zhongdian, where we used a minibus for our travels, and the much more adventurous and strenuous camping trek on the Mekong-Salween divide, where we relied on a team of ponymen and their mules to carry our baggage and equipment.

We referred to ourselves as The BNNZ Expedition, for we had members from several parts of Britain – Ronald and Joan Davey from Scotland, Roy Carter and Eileen and myself from England and Roger and Dorothy Brehaut from Guernsey: from Norway we had Gunnar and Ingebjorg Gilberg, with Andrew Young, joining us at Bangkok, from New Zealand.

Our Chinese hosts were led by Mr Xie Jinkang, whom I had met in Lijiang the pre-vious year. Our interpreter was a recently qualified graduate in English at Chengdu University. Her name was Zhang Wen but we called her Stephanie, the English name she adopted during the period of her studies (see fig.3). We had three other Chinese from the Chengdu Academy of Sciences, and our kitchen staff who had been with us in 1994.

We arrived at Kunming to be met by our hosts who laid on a splendid banquet on the evening of 28 May. An early start the next day was necessary for the 12-hour over-land journey by minibus to Dali, where we reached our hotel long after nightfall.

After inspecting the pagodas of Dali the next day we made the first of two visits to the Cangshan – a mountain range running north to south, to the west of the city. The journey by minibus took an hour, during which we saw many flowers and plants which excited us. At a convenient place for turning the bus around, we alighted and descended the track on foot, botanizing as we went. None of us were affected by the altitude as we quickly became engrossed in the many plant finds.

We spent the whole of the next day on the Cangshan, leaving the minibus where we had done the day before, but this time climbing up as far as time and the path would allow. Unfortunately rock blasting was in progress on the main track to the TV station so we were unable to reach the area where, in the previous year, I had discovered 16 different rhododendron species.

We took a lesser path in the opposite direction and climbed to a height of 3,000m (9,800ft). Our finds over the two days on the Cangshan were: *R. arboreum* subsp. *delavayi, R. aberconwayi, R. brachyanthum, R. crassum, R. davidsonianum, R. decorum, R. edgeworthii, R. maddenii, R. microphyton, R. neriiflorum, R. polyandrum* (Subsect. Maddenia), *R. rigidum, R. racemosum, R. scabrifolium* and *R. yunnanense.*

Maybe some eyebrows will be raised as to the authenticity of *R. maddenii* and *R. polyandrum* on this list. Both species are listed in the *Flora of China* from which they were keyed out, unless of course recent reclassification has lumped them with number 4 on the list. Our observations showed them to be very different, within the limited means at our disposal. Among the 45 other species of plants we listed, especially were noted *Deutzia calycosa, Iris delavayi, Piptanthus concolor, Pleione yunnanensis* and *Rodgersia pinnata.*

On 1 June we travelled to Lijiang where we reached our hotel in late afternoon. The only rhododendron of note during the day was *R. decorum* in flower on the hillsides near where we stopped to photograph Yu-Long-Shan, in the shadow of which lies the city of Lijiang, which I was delighted to see is being re-built in the old style, following the very extensive damage suffered in the earthquake of February 1996. The following day we explored the Gang-Ho-Ba, a dried up river bed at this time of the year but with many interesting plants in the valley sides as well as over the floor, situated about 40 minutes drive north of the city. Here the plants we found were: *R. cuneatum, R. decorum, R. telmateium, R. vernicosum* surprisingly growing in limestone rubble and *R. yunnanense.*

Among the 46 other plants listed, of special note were *Androsace spinulifera, Berberis temolaica, Cypripedium margaritaceum, C. tibeticum, Meconopsis delavayi* and *Primula forrestii.*

In the morning of our second day in Lijiang we visited the Temple of 1000 Camellias and enjoyed the relaxation of a gentle stroll through the grounds. For me personally this was the chance to renew my acquaintance with the chief lama and present him with a photograph. As on previous occasions, he made us very welcome and we much enjoyed the traditional tasting of walnuts and honey. In the afternoon we visited the old city which has not lost any of its character in spite of the severe damage caused by the earthquake.

The next day we journeyed in our bus to Zhongdian, making several stops en route to photograph the Yangtse River and two rhododendron species spectacular when seen *en masse* – *R. yunnanense* in mixed open woodland for miles along the valley sides, and *R. racemosum* on the open plateau as we approached Zhongdian.

In the morning of our first day based at Zhongdian we explored the ridge above Napa-Hai, and what a floral feast we enjoyed. In three visits to this area I have never before seen such a display of rhododendrons in flower. It would seem that the tendency to biennial flowering that occurs with our plants in cultivation, also happens in the wild. The plants we found were: *R. aganniphum, R. arboreum* subsp. *delavayi, R. balfourianum, R. chryseum, R. coriaceum, R. decorum, R. pachytrichum, R. vernicosum, R. wardii, R. yunnanense* and a clear hybrid of *R. vernicosum* × *R. wardii*, with flowers of an apricot colour, and its parents growing on either side. The only other plant of note was an extensive ground covering of *Androsace rigida*.

The maximum altitude we achieved was 3,600m (11,800ft) with no problems. In the afternoon we visited a spectacular ravine in the hills to the south of the city. The Chinese refer to part of its rock formation as the 'Fair Lady', so we named it 'The Fair Lady Ravine'. Although we did see a few plants of *R. adenogynum, R. primuliflorum* and *R. telmateium,* these were, however, insignificant compared with the drifts of *Primula polyneura* and *P. deflexa, Meconopsis prattii, Corydalis pachycentra, Daphne calcicola,* and in pride of place, *Paraquilegia anemonoides*. Many plants of the last were growing in the vertical cliff faces and we photographed one with 33 flowers, a truly magnificent sight. In this ravine we found plants from 29 genera with several different species each in many of them. Very sadly we saw much evidence of possible damage or destruction of the ravine, at its entrance, either by quarrying or the building of a power station.

The next day we visited Beta-Hai and explored the river valley which runs eastwards from the hamlet. At once we noticed the difference in the vegetation due to the damper conditions, compared with the previous morning on the ridge – exposed and dry – at Napa-Hai. Here were primulas in abundance and great variety, and *Rhododendron hippophaeoides*, which is well known for requiring more moisture than many in the genus. In general however the flowering of the rhododendrons in this location was poor compared to 1996. The concept of biennial flowering was thus further exemplified and our knowledge tested to the full as we had to key out the identity of our finds from foliage alone: *R. adenogynum, R. callimorphum, R. chryseum, R. decorum, R. detonsum, R. hippophaeoides* both blue and pink flowering forms, *R. oreotrephes, R. racemosum, R. selense* and *R. vernicosum*.

Two other plants of note were *Cynoglossum* species with black flowers and *Meconopsis pseudointegrifolia*.

After lunch we travelled northwards along the road leading to the village of Weng-sui, hoping to see *R. trichostomum*. Our hopes were in vain but we were compensated by a floral feast, almost all along the roadside for mile upon mile, of rhododendrons, chiefly *R. decorum* and *R. yunnanense*. One other plant equally outstanding and also at the roadside was a drift of *Podophyllum* with deep pink flowers which appear before the foliage, itself very attractive being heavily blotched and spotted with brown and red.

Tianchi Lake and its environs was our site of exploration for our last day at Zhongdian. The lake is situated at an altitude of 3,700m (12,200ft) in the hills to the south of the city. After leaving the bus we climbed through a forest on a steep hillside littered with dead and fallen trees which had been attacked by a beetle – not on this occasion by man's activities. The effect was to have let

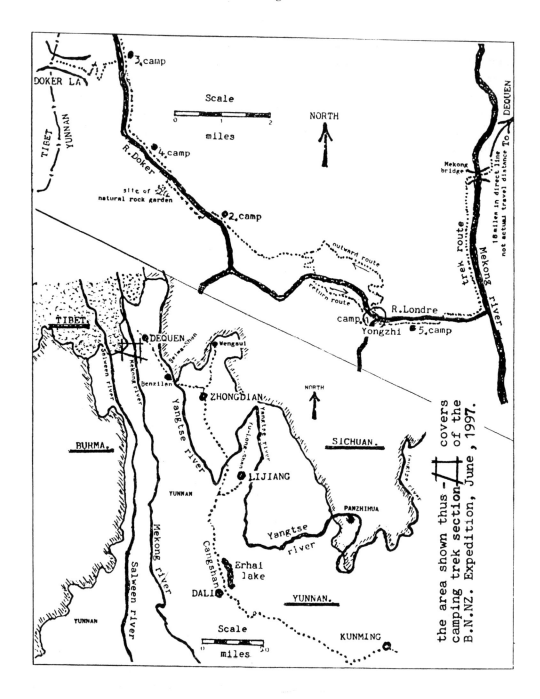

BNNZ expedition to Yunnan

more light into the area and we saw regeneration of many herbaceous and shrubby plants, including rhododendrons. *R. heliolepis* was unmistakable with its leaf scales so large that it was hardly necessary to use a magnifying glass to identify them. Two areas of 'blue' drew most attention – the first was *R. hippophaeoides* in a hollow covering about an acre and the second of even greater extent where we may have identified nine species of Lapponica, but such was the variation that some may have been natural hybrids. The nine species were: *R. fastigiatum, R. impeditum, R. intricatum, R. nivale, R. orthocladum, R. russatum, R. scintillans, R. tapetiforme* and *R. telmateium.*

Other rhododendrons found were *R. aganniphum, R. adenogynum, R. beesianum, R. chryseum, R. racemosum, R. wardii* and *R. yunnanense.* This last named was also seen *en masse* covering a hillside on the other side of the valley as we drove back to the Zhongdian plain.

Plants from other genera noted included: *Arisaema* species – the first of many we were to see later on the trip; *Mandragora caulescens* with its black, pulsatilla-like flowers; *Meconopsis pseudointegrifolia* (with its large yellow flowers); *Primula* – five species of which *P. boreiocalliantha* was the most interesting as it prefers to grow under the cover of rhododendrons (a good companion plant).

The journey northward from Zhongdian to Dequen took us through some of the most spectacular and majestic scenery as we travelled along the Yangtse Gorge towards Beima-Shan, the 4,875m (16,000ft) mountain which overlooks the high pass at 4,300m (14,100ft), beginning the long descent to Dequen.

Next morning, 9 June, a two-hour journey on the minibus took us from Dequen down to the Mekong River – a descent of nearly 1,220m (4,000ft) on a narrow track with passing places. For most of the journey we were tucked in between near vertical high cliffs on the one side and equally vertical precipitous drops on the other with no parapet along the edge, although, happily, we had an excellent driver. At the bridge we were met by the ponymen and I was delighted that four of them, who had been with us in 1994, were there again. We set off across the narrow suspension bridge to walk to Yongzhi via the gorge of a tributary of the Mekong, where in places the rock walls were so sheer that our path had been carved out of the rock face, with the raging torrent tens of metres below spectacular but not a place for the faint-hearted! Our first camp site was in the farmyard at Yongzhi (Londre in Kingdon-Ward time) and it seemed that the whole village turned out to welcome us and assist with pitching tents, unpacking kitbags and helping our kitchen staff.

Next day we reached camp two in late afternoon after climbing just over 1,070m (3,500ft). Many plants were noticed en route but little serious botanizing was done as our main preoccupation was the steep ascent. The first rhododendron seen was *R. decorum* at about 2,750m (9,000ft), but few plants were flowering – it will be interesting to see the amount of flower in 1998 to check the concept of biennial flowering if, as seems likely, I am invited to lead another group of first-timers to the same region. We took things easy the next day. In the morning an hour's walk along a very rough track through

the forest brought us to an extensive plantation of *R. edgeworthii*. In the afternoon,
having retraced our steps to lunch at the
camp, we wandered northward and climbing
through the forest came upon a fantastic
sight which could only be described as an
Arisaema forest, with the greatest concentra-
tion of at least 50 plants in an area no bigger
than that of a tennis court. In the course of
our wanderings we spotted *R. anthosphaerum*
of the Irroratum Subsect., but it had long
since finished flowering, and also *R.
diaprepes* with no flowers.

We were advised by the head ponyman
that many flowers were to be seen if we continued northwards towards the famous
mountain pass – the Doker La – so on the
morning of 12 June we broke camp and pro-
ceeded through the *Arisaema* forest and
onwards and upwards, at first through forest
and later into more open country, always
close to a river or stream as this is how
ancient routes were developed, of course. In
the forest section we were excited to find a
large plant of that curious member of our
genus, *R. genestierianum* while further on as
the trees thinned and the high mountains
appeared we came across a natural rock
garden in which 14 species, at least, of
rhododendrons were all growing, in a fairly
recent rock fall, in an area of no more than
0.4ha (1 acre). The rock fall had obviously
brought down from higher altitude a
number of the species to mix with those
already growing on the high alpine meadow,
through which our path led us. Our identification of the 14 was: *R. brachyanthum, R.
calostrotum, R. cephalanthum, R. chame-
unum, R. chryseum, R. forrestii, R. heliolepis,
R. hypolepidotum, R. mekongense, R.

*oreotrephes, R. primuliflorum, R. saluenense,
R. sanguineum* and *R. tapetiforme.*

It is now understood that *R. brachyanthum* and *R. hypolepidotum* are variants of
the same species but the plants we saw were
very different in several aspects and are listed
separately in the *Flora of China.*

Another two hours walking, during
which I found two more rhododendrons
new on the trip – *R. fulvoides* and *R. uvarifolium*, brought us to the foot of the Doker
La, which in fact extends westwards at right
angles to the main valley up which we had
walked. The following day we only climbed
further up the main valley, and saw nothing
new, with the exception of *R. temenium*,
which gains its name from a sacred place
near the Doker La.

In the dawn light the next day mist
swirled around the many high peaks, and
then as this lifted we could see a panorama
of mountains which appeared to encircle us
completely (see fig. 4). We ate a hasty break-
fast and set off to climb the Doker La, which
in geographical terms, has the appearance of
a hanging valley. It was generally a poor
flowering season for rhododendrons – one
hillside was covered with *R. flavorufum*, with
its distinctive leaf indumentum, but I saw
only one in flower. It was an excitement to
see on the distant skyline, the summit of the
pass, and the two Norwegian members of
our party managed to reach it over the snow
– a splendid achievement.

After a leisurely return to camp four the
following day, we crossed the river, where we
split into two groups. My group came across
a huge area full of *Primula sikkimensis* – like
a field of buttercups in an English meadow.
The other group, after a very stiff two hour

climb, discovered a hidden high meadow of *R. forrestii* fully in flower, and extending to an area of at least 0.4ha (1 acre). After this, the climax of our trip, we were homeward bound. A long day's march and a steep descent took us back to camp five, midway between the village of Yongzhi and the Mekong bridge, where the following day we said farewell to the ponymen, whose families, in colourful traditional dress, had turned out to greet them. From there we returned to Lijiang, where we attended a concert of local Naxi music, given by a largely septuagenerian orchestra playing on ancient instruments, and conducted by Dr Xuan Ke. He lives in the house once occupied by Dr Joseph Rock, and next day he invited us to see his library and his memoribilia of Joseph Rock. From Lijiang we flew to Kunming, and from there home.

DAVID FARNES *has been a member of the Group's Executive Committee since 1978 and is Branch Organiser of the Peak District Branch. He has been on several expeditions to China*

Rhododendron yakushimanum Hybrids – The End of the Line?

John Bond

I wonder if there is a serious rhododendron enthusiast who would not place *Rhododendron degronianum* subsp. *yakushimanum* (please note that I am 'toeing the line' concerning nomenclature) in the top 10 rhododendron species. It would certainly be among the elite of my list and certainly very close to the top.

It would appear unnecessary to extol the virtues of *R. yakushimanum* to readers of this august publication. However, I intend to do that to complete the picture for or against hybridization. Incidentally, I dislike the abbreviation 'yak'. First, the foliage, and I invariably consider the foliage of rhododendrons before the flower, which is superb on a well-grown specimen for 12 months, and an additional outstanding bonus for several weeks when the young growth appears. Secondly, the flowers are so very pretty. Apple blossom is my description of the colour, a quiet colouring that appeals to me immensely. The species, having reached an age of five or six years, will flower freely every year, providing deadheading is practised immediately after flowering. Thirdly, the species, or more correctly the sub species, is both heat and cold tolerant, for as we are

all aware it hails from the exposed mountain tops of Yakushima Island. Fourthly, this is an extremely useful rhododendron for the smaller garden attaining in 20 years 1.2-1.5m × 1.5-2m (4-5ft × 5-6ft). If you are gardening on a larger scale plant a group of six or seven. One last point on the virtues of the species, if you bend the rules and place a specimen in half shade or even a little more instead of in its rightful place in full exposure the general appearance of the specimen will change dramatically. Specimens will attain 2m (6ft) or even 2.5m (8ft) quickly, produce larger but still very attractive foliage on a somewhat more lax shrub, and finer but fewer flowers. Worth considering perhaps?

Of all the many wild collectings of this species that I have seen, none have equalled the quality of the First Class Certificate form which has been given the clonal name 'Koichiro Wada'. In fact, some years ago Jelena de Belder from Kalmthout Arboretum, Belgium, gave me 50 superb plants of a range of seedlings raised from seed they had collected in 1970 on Yakushima at high altitude from very tight low growing plants. Lovely as these plants now are, they did not retain a dwarf character and the one FCC specimen I planted among them stands out as being clearly superior.

The account of the first two plants to be sent to Britain, Exbury in fact, in 1934 has always interested me and to a point amazed me; particularly the fact that the two plants survived the considerable military activity at Exbury during the Second World War, eventually making a debut at Vincent Square in 1947. Perhaps further proof of the ease of cultivation and value of the species?

So there you are; providing the soil is acid and in fair order *R. yakushimanum* will grow and flourish almost anywhere in the world and provide the enthusiast with the greatest of pleasure.

And now to the point of this paper. If this species is so wonderful and it clearly is, why use it as a parent for hybridization? Following that question, we should ask ourselves why we make hybrids and I can immediately hear a great cry – to improve upon the parents – to produce new and better foliage, flowers, habit, etc. and my answer in the case of *R. yakushimanum* is that I am definitely unaware of the need for these improvements.

To add strength to the statement above, during the period when I was writing this paper I had occasion to judge a flower show and spend a night away from home. On the journey to the show venue, as always I took the opportunity to visit a horticultural establishment of interest. In this case, it was a near perfect garden centre and in the course of my tour of the establishment I came upon the rhododendrons. As is usual, there was a small range of dwarf hybrids and a very great selection of excellent *R. yakushimanum* hybrids. Being July there was no flower but

excellent foliage and at one end a dozen plants of *R. yakushimanum* FCC which stood out 'head and shoulders', in quality not size, over the many hybrids in the same display; proof indeed should I need proof.

Let us look then at some of the hybrids that are available; no doubt I shall miss some favourites out of my notes and there will be cries of 'What about my - - -?!' I have already shown my preference for the apple blossom colour range. It is not surprising, therefore, that I am particularly attracted to David Leach's *R.* 'Crete', *R.* 'Mist Maiden' and *R.* 'Pink Parasol' and another hybrid from the United States, *R.* 'Ken Janeck'. Several of these are registered as forms of *R. yakushimanum* but in my opinion they are without exception hybrids, almost certainly with the super hardy *R. smirnowii*. There are two or three plants which are definitely of this parentage growing in the Savill Garden which were given to me by the raiser, Gus Mehlquist, some years ago, and in the same garden an even finer hybrid of this type which was given to me by the late Donald Lowndes of MacPennys Nursery in the New Forest, also as yet unnamed. Readers will note my brief review of some of the hybrids available begins with the best, for all the above are really very pretty rhododendrons. They fall short of the species on account of their broader less attractive foliage.

The cross, *R. yakushimanum* × *R. bureavii*, has been made by a number of hybridists who were obviously seeking good foliage and this, with such good parents, they usually appear to have achieved. The influence of *R. bureavii* appears to dominate and as is normal with this species the offspring appear to be shy to flower. The American, R. 'Teddy Bear', is much in evidence in garden centres.

Rhododendron pseudochrysanthum is an obvious choice to hybridists to use and I have seen several promising results of this cross. Incidently, R. *pseudochrysanthum* is also in my top 10 best species.

Most rhododendron enthusiasts will be aware of the Waterer R. *yakushimanum* hybrids which were raised at Bagshot in the 70s and are now to be seen, often in large numbers, in every garden centre in Britain. I consider a number of these to be very pretty and acceptable in the garden. They are, however, best looked upon as useful free flowering compact hybrids with very little input from R. *yakushimanum*, at the most a quarter, and in many cases much less.

Arthur George of Hydon Nurseries has been more successful than most with his hybridizing. His glamorous free flowering progeny from 'Springbok' and R. *yakushimanum*, 'Hydon Dawn' and 'Morning Cloud' are particularly good.

The Savill and Valley Gardens have had mixed success from a variety of crosses. For good foliage, R. 'King's Ride' is difficult to beat. This has R. *insigne* as a parent which tells its own story. A very good hybrid with a pretty clear pink R. *arboreum* did not find favour when shown at Vincent Square a few years ago but the cross made with R. × *loderi* 'Sir Edmund' has been more fortunate with an FCC after trial at the RHS Garden, Wisley. This will not be dwarf, of course, and in fact the plant becomes decidedly leggy with age. A Cory Cup winner, R.

'Streatley', is the result of a cross made with R. *aberconwayi*. This is a very pretty small rhododendron attaining some 1.5m (5ft) eventually. A number of crosses were made with R. 'Hawk', R. *wardii* and R. *litiense*, with little or no real success. However, there are three plants in the Savill Garden of an excellent R. *wardii* × R. *yakushimanum* cross as yet unnamed which were propagated from scions given to me by the late Lionel Fortescue. There is very little evidence of the Japanese species apart from the domed shape of the shrub. However, the clear creamy yellow flowers are outstanding.

What do I write about Herr Hachmann's many new hybrids? They are the results of many crosses between ironclad hardy hybrids and the species, which have produced some decidedly cabbage-like foliage, and I have to say some very pretty flowers. In fact, they are a new compact race of hardy hybrids and if I gardened in cold northern Europe with little or no maritime influence I should be more than grateful.

So what do we do to deter future hybridists of R. *yakushimanum*? Nothing, of course, for there is obviously no law against it and I do not suggest that we picket rhododendron meetings world-wide with placards asking keen hybridists to stop.

I do ask, however, that hybridists give considerable thought to future efforts.

JOHN BOND *is the new Chairman of the Group's Executive Committee and a member of RHS Council. He has recently retired as Keeper of the Gardens, Windsor Great Park*

THE HARDY GHENT AZALEAS

ALBERT DE RAEDT

It would not be modern botanical practice to describe under one collective name, a group of plants whose origin is so varied as the 'Hardy Ghent' azaleas. We speak about mollis, viscosum or occidentale hybrids where, in each case, one of these species is a parent. The 'Hardy Ghents', however, are the product of crossings between at least five distinct species – *R. calendulaceum*, *R. flammeum* (*Azalea speciosa*), *R. peryclymenoides* (*A. nudiflora*), *R. prinophyllum* (*A. rosea*), *R. viscosum* and *R. luteum* (*A. pontica*). Subsequently *R. molle* (*A. sinensis*) and in some cases *R. occidentale*, were also successfully used. Some examples today of the first group would be 'Daviesii', 'Unique', and 'Nancy Waterer', and of the second, 'Magnificum', and 'Magnificum Albicans'. It should be noted, incidentally, that there is also an occidentale hybrid named 'Magnificum'.

Contrary to what the group name, 'Hardy Ghents', might indicate, Ghent in Belgium was not the only place where these azaleas were hybridized, but it was, very probably, the first. The original hybridization seems to have been undertaken at the beginning of the 19th century, by an amateur grower, P Mortier (1768-1847), who was a baker by profession. His hybrids named *Azalea mortieriana*, *A. mortierii*, or by other variants of his name. At a later date,

he crossed his hybrids with the yellow flowered hardy and sweet scented *R. luteum* (*A. pontica*). It was the resulting plants that became known as 'Harde Ghentse azaleas', 'Azalées rustiques de Gand', or 'Hardy Ghents'; or in the Netherlands and Germany, as 'Pontica hybrids'.

In 1834 Mortier sold his last hybrids to the nurseryman Louis Verschaffelt. At about the same period a Mr Gowen on behalf of the Earl of Carnarvon at Highclere, in the county of Berkshire, England, must have made crossings with the Mortier hybrids. He too used *R. molle* and *R. viscosum*. Less well known are the crosses made by a Herr Rinz in Germany. In about 1833 he seems to have succeeded in crossing Mortier's hybrids and *A. pontica* 'Flora Albo Pleno'. I doubt if any present day connoisseur has knowledge of this azalea, but that is how it was described in *Gartenflora* of 1854. That description states that from these crossings 12 (all doubles) were selected, but only two were mentioned by name. These were 'Graf von Meran' and 'Chromatella', as indeed they are still known to this day. In 1855 Ambroise Verschaffelt, who in 1850 had succeeded to the business of his father Alexander, the brother of the Louis Verschaffelt already mentioned, published a list of 11 double flowered 'Hardy Ghents', stating that they came from Germany. It was only later that the name of Rinz was mentioned.

In France also, there were, quite early on, some growers who contributed to the abundance of new varieties that flooded the market. It is a pity that, as yet, we have been unable to discover adequate documentation. However, it is possible to quote some of the names, such as Sénéclause with 'Coccineum Speciosum' and 'Gloria Mundi', Quihou with 'Fritz Quihou' (a fine red); Croux and Moser.

In 1846 a first list of 12 hybrids ascribed to M L Verschaffelt was published, in Belgium, in the *Annales de la Société Royale d'Agriculture et de Botanique de Gand* where they were still referred to as *A. mortieriana* (*mortierii*) var *hybridae*. The following year a further 8 were added. In his pricelist of 1849 Louis Van Houtte writes that he is offering 25 new varieties, styled the Louis Verschaffelt collection. Table C compares the Van Houtte list with the two *Annales* lists of 1846 and 47. The cultivars printed **bold** in the Van Houtte list have survived in collections to the present day. If one compares the two lists one finds that some cultivars had been renamed. There exist also the lithos of 1846 (see fig. 4) and 1847, exactly as originally published in the *Annales*.

In 1855 the *Illustration Horticole* published, also in colour, 16 new hardy Ghents together with 10 double-flowered hybrids. These are described in Table A, and again those cultivars known to be still in cultivation are shown in **bold**.

In 1873 the *Flore des Serres et des Jardins de l'Europe, tome XIX*, published by Louis Van Houtte, contained a description of 12 new hardy Ghents, among them 6 (including a colour reproduction) he says he obtained from the widow of a Louis Hellebuyck. It said that this grower, by tenacious crossing and selection from thousands of seedlings, that had *A. pontica* as the mother plant, and as male parent one of several species from the eastern United States (*A. calendulaceae, A. nudiflora, A. viscosa*, and *A. bicolour*), had produced the following six azaleas. Again those cultivars known to be still in cultivation are shown in **bold**.

Louis Hellebuyck; Mad. Alex Hardy; **Mina Van Houtte**; **Louis A. Van Houtte**; Francois de Taye; **Bijou de Gentebruggen**.

In pricelist no. 174 of 1877, 12 'nouveautés' were mentioned, unclassified but under the name 'Van Houtte' - Francois De Taye; **Bijou de Ghentbrugge**; **Mina van Houtte**; **Louis Aime van Houtte**; **Louis Hellebuyck**; Mad. Alex Hardy; **Rose de Flandre**; **Domenico Scassi** ; Dr. Auguste Cambier; Fidele Mechelynck; **Sang de Gentbrugge**.

Only in the 1870s did it become customary to present the different cultivars with a colour description, descriptions with commercial intentions that were not always uniform and certainly not always accurate. Colour numbers as we use them now were unknown at that time. From the various pricelists, discovered in different libraries by a fellow member of the Belgian Dendrological Society, Leon Declerq, it has been possible to gather together a list of almost 1,000 different names, although certainly including a number of synonyms. Mostly names are given without a colour description, but these are known for 600 cultivars.

The next phase of the investigation,

undertaken originally by Leon Declerq, and subsequently also by J Delvaux and myself, consisted of endeavouring to trace which cultivars were still available and where they were located. So far we have had success in Belgium at the Arboretum in Kalmthout, at the Castle in Beervelde, and, of course in Leon Declerq's own garden; in Germany in the Rhododendronpark at Bremen and at the show garden of the Horticultural Institute at Bad Zwischenahn; in England at the beautiful collections at the RHS Garden, Wisley, the Sir Harold Hillier Arboretum, the National Trust Garden at Sheffield Park, Sussex, and the Royal Botanic Gardens, Kew. Unfortunately most of the plants in these collections are not labelled. Our information about collections in France and the Netherlands is very scarce. The only well known specialised commercial nursery, through the assistance of Leon Declerq, is the nursery De Keyser - Matthijs, which is situated at Lochristi, near Ghent. In total we have, so far, recorded on computer 135 cultivars held in 20 public or private gardens, in Belgium, Germany, the United Kingdom and the USA.

Closely related to the 'Hardy Ghents' are the 'Rustica' azaleas. The situation of this group of deciduous azaleas is totally different, for the following reasons. We know exactly when they were brought onto the market, that is by a single nursery in the period 1888-1900; they are all double flowered and sweet scented. And yet here also we find many unanswered questions. Charles Vuylsteke of Lochristi showed his novelties (probably 18) for the first time in Ghent in 1888. However we have been unable to trace his pricelist. He called them 'Azalea Rustica

Flore Pleno', and also '*Azalea mollis*', 'Hybrides a fleurs doubles'.

The fact that Vuylsteke uses the description *A. mollis* hybride (i.e. *R. japonicum*) suggests that there is another species or cultivar involved, but which one? Here is a much larger problem. Vuylsteke probably did not know himself which was the other parent, as he had not carried out the crossing and selection of the 18 himself. This had been done by a Louis De Smet, but he had since died, and exactly like Mortier 60 years earlier, he had told no one which crossings he had made. It is quite probable that he had made crossings unsystematically with several species. Some think that he may have crossed *R. japonicum* with *R. occidentale* or with an Occidentalis hybrid. But this would not produce double flowered specimens. It is almost certain that a double 'Hardy Ghent' must have been involved as the mother plant (because they seldom or never have stamens).

There are also different views about the assortment. In Vuylsteke's offer as printed of 1913, there were 26 different cultivars, numbered 400 to 426. The numbers 400 to 417 are the same as the original offer of 1888. The next 5 are believed to have been added later on. 'Teniers', 'Quentin Metsys', 'Corneille', 'Racine', and 'Fenelon', are all still in our gardens. No. 424 'Dyogine' was offered only once by Vuylsteke, and was never offered by any other nurseryman. In *Rhododendrons and Azaleas* by H Grootendorst (published 1954), it is stated that only the first 18 can be considered as Rusticas and that the remainder belong to the double 'Hardy Ghents', because they produce too many leaves and show too vigorous a growth. However neither Ch. Vuylsteke nor any of his colleagues made such a distinction.

The only cultivars on the 1900 list it has not been possible to identify in current cultivation, up to the present moment , are Nos 418 and 419, 'Rubens' and 'Van Dyck'. The mistake should not be made of confusing these two 'Rusticas' with the 'Hardy Ghents' of the same names on the list published in 1846 (Table C). Finally, Table B illustrates the complete list as printed in 1913.

Albert De Raedt lives near Ghent in Belgium and is a member of the Belgian Dendrological Society. He is preparing a book on Hardy Ghent Azaleas for publication

---

TABLE A
from Illustration Horticole 1855

AZALÉES DE PLEINE TERRE

Collection nouvelle

Atrorubens nova	Duc d'Ursel	Nobilis
Baron G. Pyke	**Eugénie**	Richardii
Beauté de Flandres	Honneur de la Belgique	Rosea formisissima
Delicata Nova	Magnifica Albicans	Rosea lineata
	Miniata Floribunda	Rosea rotundiflora
	Néron	**Rubra splendidissima**

Collection nouvelle a fleurs doubles

Arethusa	cream white
Bartolo Lazza	deep brick red
Dr Streiter	deep yellow
Graf von Meran	soft rose
Heroine	flesh coloured
Leibnitz	golden yellow to bright red
Maja	brick red
Narcissiflora	pale yellow
Ophirie	bright yellow
Rosetta	pure white streaked rose

The cultivars shown in **bold** are those still existing in collections

---

TABLE B

AZALEA RUSTICA FLORE PLENO

400 Adriane	409 Mecene	418 Rubens
401 Aida	410 Norma	419 Van Dyk
402 Apelles	411 Phoebe	421 Teniers
403 Murillo	412 Virgile	422 Q Metsya
404 Il Tasso	413 Phidias	423 Corneille
405 Freya	414 Le Titien	424 Dyogine
406 Hora	415 Praxitele	425 Racine
407 Ribera	416 Byron	426 Fenelon
408 Velasquez	417 Milton	

TABLE C

L. VERSCHAFFELT 1846-7		L. VAN HOUTTE 1849	
NAME	DESCRIPTION	NAME	DESCRIPTION
Prince Henri des Pays-Bas	Orange red flower, one lobe yellow, fiery	**Prince Henri des Pays-Bas**	Fiery orange; one lobe yellow; very bright shade
Orange peinte	Yellow base; purple edge; one lobe without edge	**Guillaume II**	Basically yellow; purple edge; lobe without edging; tips white; first rate
Triomphe de Royghem	Flower rose, central yellow strip; edge redder; lobe completely yellow, red at the edge	Triomphe de Royghem	Rose; centre of upper lobe yellow with red surround central strip of other lobes pale yellow
Reine d'Angleterre	Flower rose, central strip of Isabel yellow	Reine d'Angleterre	Rose; lobes with Isabel yellow strips
Marie-Dorothée	Flower completely white one lobe pale Isabel yellow	Marie-Dorothée	Completely white flower except one bright Isabel yellow lobe; rose streaks
Florentina	Flower completely rose; central strip white and pale Isabel yellow	Florentine	Rose with the centre strips white and Isabel yellow; one lobe orange; first rate
Grand-Duc	Flower flesh colour; central strip pale; lobe nankeen yellow	Grand-Duc de Luxembourg	Fleshy red; central strip brighter; one lobe nankeen yellow
Quadricolore	Flower basically nankeen yellow; flame red on Isabel yellow, one lobe orange	**Quadricolore**	Basically nankeen yellow, some flame on Isabel yellow; one lobe orange; first rate
Cardinal	Dark rose basically edge redder, yellow lobe	**Admiraal de Ruyter**	Dark rose tube; redder edging; one lobe yellow
Minerve	Rose flower; yellow lobe	Minerve	Silky rose; one lobe nankin; lilac and bronze sheen; large flower
Van Dyck	Bright purple flower; single coloured	Van Dyck	Bright purple single coloured; first rate
Rubens	The same but one lobe yellow	Rubens	Same basic colour but one lobe chrome yellow; large flower; first rate
Oscar premier	Purple rose flower; upper divisions brilliant yellow edged with deep purple; this variety is magnificent	**Oscar ler**	Rose purple flower; upper divisions brilliant yellow edged with dark purple
Etendard	Dark purple flower; one lobe flesh coloured	Etendard	Dark purple flower; one lobe fleshy red; first rate
Rosalie	Soft pink flower washed with yellow and with a pink edge	Rosalie	Soft rose flower washed yellow and edged rose
Gloire de Verschaffelt	Bright purple flower; each division with a rose stripe; the lower lobe lightly washed with yellow; white streaks	Gloire de Verschaffelt	Bright purple flower; each division with a rose stripe; the lower lobe lightly washed yellow; white streaks
Spigelius	Pale rose flower, flushed with yellow and one lobe entirely yellow	**Sully**	Bright rose; a pure yellow stripe; band; standard orange; large flower
Le rayon du matin	Completely golden yellow flower with a paler ray	Princesse d'Orange	Brilliant golden yellow; large flower; first rate
Le perle du Printemps	Flower with three of the corolla divisions yellow, edged with rose	Perle du Printemps	Rose flower; three of the corolla divisions yellow, with the edge rose; large flower; first rate
Le soupir du crépuscule	Yellow flower, with a brick red edge; one division darker yellow	**Cymodocée**	Sulphur yellow, with the edge red with a touch of Massaka
Général Chassé	Dark orange red; extra	**Général Chassé**	Dark orange red; first rate
		Jules César	Crimson; large flower
		Souvenir de Mortier	Rose mixed with dark red; first rate
		Bronze Unique	Dark red with a touch of bronze; first rate
		Sinensis Striata	Bright rose streaked with white

The cultivars shown **bold** are those still existing in collections and those underlined have a name change in the later list.

FURTHER RHODODENDRON HUNTING IN VIETNAM

KEITH RUSHFORTH

Since my article in the 1993 Year Book, I have made two further trips to Vietnam, both with Dr David Chamberlain and both excellently organised by Professor Dr Trân Cong Khánh of the Hanoi College of Pharmacy. In November 1994 with Peta and Vinh Burton Smith we visited Sapa and Dalat. The March/April 97 trip (with David's wife Maria, Janet Cubey and Claire Shanks) was intended to explore two southern peaks before heading back to the Sapa region to sort out some remaining conundra there. The weather this spring was much wetter than normal (we had planned to be in the south during the dry season!). As a result, we only half conquered Bidoup and decided to leave Ngoc Linh to next time. The numbers in square brackets refer to the numbering used in my 1993 article.

However, the south is new territory and I will start there. In both 1994 and 1997 we climbed to the top of Langbian (12.02′44.5″N, 108.26′28.72″E, 2,167m/ 7,110ft), an isolated peak some 11.3km (7 miles) north of DàLat in Lâm Dông province, and which is the type locality of two rhododendron species. The mountain rises some 600m (1,970ft) above the general level of the (undulating) plateau and comprises two peaks. The main summit is some

250m (820ft) higher than the adjacent col. I have not visited the second peak, which I estimate (from the top of the main peak) as perhaps 50m (165ft) lower, with a rounded top, and (which is crucial) apparently no rocky outcrop as is found on the main peak.

The lower slopes of Langbian are dominated by *Pinus kesiya* forest with *Mahonia annamica* among other recognizable plants. At the level of the col, evergreen tropical montane forest begins, with trees such as tan oaks (*Lithocarpus*) and *Elaeocarpus*, plus the occasional *Podocarpus*. On the western side of Langbian this forest continues up to the summit, acquiring two species of maple (*Acer heptaphlebum* and *A. erythanthum*), a *Magnolia* or two and *Prunus* among other plants (the *Dichroa febrifuga* is particularly stunning with its turquoise fruits). At the top of this slope is a narrow zone of forest dominated by *Rhododendron langbianense*, with *Sorbus granulosa*. The zone has an altitudinal range of perhaps 30m (100ft) and a linear extent of perhaps 100m (330ft). *R. langbianense* forms trees up to 10m (30ft) in height and they seem to flower during the dry season, starting in November and finishing around February. *R. langbianense* appears just hardy. I had one outside last winter when we had below freezing temperatures for about 18 days after Christmas (although not exceptionally low ones); this came into leaf but I think the roots rotted off and I have since lost it. Ted Millais had two batches each of a score of plants in an unheated polytunnel – with one plant of each batch surviving the frosts at Churt, Surrey. *R. langbianense* is a form or relative of *R. irroratum*, but appears not to be the same as *R. kontumense* which is where David placed it in his revision.

Growing as an epiphyte on *R. langbianense* and also on moss covered rocks is *R. triumphans*. This is a beautiful true Vireya species with large red flowers, and was first described from near Nhatrang, some 97km (60 miles) to the east.

The third species on Langbian is *R. fleuryi*. It is only known for certain from this peak, but may occur on other sufficiently high peaks in the locality, such as Bidoup and Chu Yang Sin (the reference to Laos in the Edinburgh revision is one of those annoying errors which creep in). *R. fleuryi* is perhaps the rarest and most threatened of any species I have seen, exceeding the vulnerability of *Picea martinezii* in Mexico. It is restricted to the open rocky hillside on the northwestern corner of the peak, in an area perhaps 20-30m (70-100ft) in length with an altitudinal range of circa 15m (50ft). In this habitat, there are no more than half a dozen mature trees, to 6m (20ft), with basal stem diameters to 20cm (8in), and a good number of seedlings. The bark is exquisite, flaking mahogany, while the flowers are nearly white. The leaves are unusually dark and densely scaly beneath. Since 1994, at least one mature plant has been destroyed to make a campfire on the open grassy knoll of

the summit. Occurring on Langbian with the *R. fleuryi* was a *Hypericum* species of equally restricted distribution. In 1994 there were four plants of the *Hypericum* on the summit, but these have since been burnt off and it is now only present on the same restricted area as the *R. fleuryi*.

We had permission to visit Bidoup (12.08'05.7"N, 108.39'14.5"E, 2,287m/ 7,503ft), located in a line between Dalat and Nhatrang and some 32km (20 miles) east of Langbian, but only to spend one night on the mountain. Unfortunately, due to the wet weather the 'road' was difficult and the journey (in the back of a lorry) took over six hours each way, leaving little time on the mountain. The crest appears from the south to be horseshoe shaped and we were able to get only half way round towards the top. We found one rocky outcrop on which were two *Sorbus granulosa*, several *R. langbianense* and epiphytic *R. triumphans*. More *R. langbianense* occurred further along the ridge, among trees of *Fokienia hodginsii* (with wonderful shaggy bark) which were majestic emergents above the general level of the forest. At least one other *Rhododendron* occurs on the mountain (which could be *R. fleuryi*), along with *Manglietia fordiana*(?), *Carpinus poilanei* and *Acer garretii*, plus the other two maples from Langbian. Further investigation will have to await the next trip . . . Any takers for a trip in February/March 1999?

While the south presents its own challenges, more investigation is still needed in the north, and my fourth trip to Sapa and its environs still leaves several puzzles. We made some progress on the taxa in Subsect. Irrorata, confirming the presence of *R. spanotrichum* [6-8] on both Suoi Doi

Location of Vietnamese Mountains Visited

Map showing the location of the Vietnamese mountains visited in 1997

(22.22′24.0″N, 103.46′40.7″E) and Fan Si Pan (22.18′10.9″N, 103.46′31.1″E), on both mountains at around 2,100m (6,890ft). This species has delightful cherry red flowers with pale whitish centres in a flat topped truss. The other confirmed member of this group is *R. tanastylum* [6-8], this being found on Fan Si Pan between about

2,400m (7,875ft) and 2,700m (8,860ft) (see fig. 8). The form on Fan Si Pan has been named *R. petelotii*. The type specimen of *R. petelotii* is poor but appears identical with the specimens from western Yunnan. The flowers are bright blood red and in perfect domed trusses. It appears to be hardy in yellow flowers, placing it in the series of

Fareham, Hampshire.

However, while these two species are confirmed, there appears to be at least one other species in this alliance on Suoi Doi, but this has not been found in flower in the wild. A seedling has flowered in Fareham but does not fit any known species and seems intermediate between Subsect.s Irrorata and Parishia. It could be part of the primordial genepool from which both sections have derived; but it could be a hybrid!

In Parishia [6-8], there are also two or three taxa, although only one has been found in flower. This is on Fan Si Pan from 2,700m (8,860ft) to the summit at 3,143m (10,312ft). The flowers are blood red in flat topped trusses which indicate some relationship with *R. facetum*. The leaves are much smaller than in *R. facetum* and more abruptly pointed. It is possible that it is just a local form of *R. facetum*, and Fan Si Pan tends to have smaller leaved forms of other species than are found on the lower and presumably less windy and more humid Suoi Doi. The leaves are similar to those of *R. huidongense*, but this white flowered species occurs in southern Sichuan, and is not known from intervening Yunnan.

The other Parishia is probably *R. facetum* itself, but it could be a form of *R. kyawii*, or perhaps both are present. It is known from roadside banks and also from the windy ridges of Suoi Doi (although Suoi Doi was the name we were given for this mountain in 1991, this name [which means 'Two Bridges' in Vietnamese] is not recognized by most locals, who appear to have no name for this peak).

The plant listed as *R.* aff. *delavayi* [4] in the 1993 account has been collected in flower and proves to be a new species (see fig. 7). It has pinky purple lopsided trusses, at its best quite attractive. The new foliage is initially brown or silvery haired above. It is widely spread from about 2,200m (7,220ft) to 2,500m (8,200ft) on both mountains.

One step forwards, two steps backwards might describe the situation with Subsect. Grandia. From the combination of juvenile and adult foliage, it appeared that the species on Suoi Doi was *R. protistum* [1] – the adult foliage fitting var. *protistum* and the juvenile plants more towards var. *giganteum*. I was not entirely convinced, and planned this spring's trip to try to get it in flower. By the time we got to climb Suoi Doi in early April from the Phong Tho road side (I have only seen a single seedling on a ridge, which has since been burnt, of Fan Si Pan above Sin Chay village) the flowers were largely over. The first tree found had a few unreachable trusses and fallen corollas underneath. These were yellow and ventricose-campanulate not funnel campanulate and pink as in *R. protistum!* However, David quickly found cup-shaped hairs, showing this as a Subsect. Falconera species. It is the unknown species recorded from Suoi Doi and Ban Khoang in 1991-92. However, rather than being unknown it is probably *R. sinofalconeri* [3] itself. This plant, therefore, did not establish the identity of the Grandia and, mainly to find better material of this *R. sinofalconeri,* we made another attempt to scale Suoi Doi, but from the Ban Khoang road! After a few false starts we managed to find the ridge I had climbed in 1991 and 1992 and where the Grandia was first found. A plant with a reachable truss showed this also has ventricose-campanulate species closely allied to *R. grande* and *R sinograde*. The flowers were rather past it, leaving room for further debate (correction, providing justification for a further visit), although I find it hard to accept it as a form of *R. sinogrande* as David has postulated. It is surprisingly hardy here, and comes into leaf late. One in the open in Fareham was battered during the 1996-97 winter but has flourished happily.

These discoveries show that there are three entities with ventricose-campanulate yellow flowers – *R.* cf. *sinogrande* [1], and two *R. sinofalconeri* taxa, 'A' [3] and 'B' [2]. The presence of two contrasting elements in *R. sinofalconeri* is noted in David's revision. The entity which fits the type is the Suoi Doi plant, which apart from the cup-shaped hairs (which define Subsect. Falconera) is virtually indistinguishable from the *R.* cf. *sinogrande* taxon. Personally I suspect that this taxon ('A') is a hybrid between the *R.* cf. *sinogrande* plant and the 'B' taxon. The 'B' taxon is common on Fan Si Pan from 2,700m (8,860ft) to the summit at 3,143m (10,312ft) and is very close to *R. falconeri* from Bhutan – with a poorer bark although the smaller leaves show off the trusses of bright yellow flowers to better effect.

The last Subgenus Hymenanthes species is another unknown. I listed it as *R.* aff. *serotinum* [5] in 1993, but David suspects it is closer to *R. chihsinianum* and *R. auriculatum*. The leaves are auricled, showing some similarity to *R. hemsleyanum* but smaller and narrower. I found a seedling in 1991 and this discovery was one of the enticements to return in the spring of 1992. Further seedlings were found along the Ban Khoang road in 1992 (and Alan Clark successfully introduced it from this roadside bank in the autumn of 1992). In 1994, some immature plants were found on a cliff face on Suoi Doi. We found more saplings this spring, but finally on a ridge of Suoi Doi (22.22'24.0"N, 103.46'40.7"E, at circa 2,490m/8,170ft) with an undergrowth of dwarf bamboo 1m (3ft) high, I found three mature 6m (20ft) plants. On this blasted ridge, the leaves were smaller and narrower than on the seedlings, and badly damaged by the exposure. There were, however, some old capsules with a few seeds remaining, as well as flower buds. Dissection of the flower buds showed that the species has a seven-lobed corolla, and lax trusses of around five to eight blooms. I thought it might flower in April, but I was wrong. From its cold ridge top site, it probably waits for the monsoon to be in full flush!

To be concluded.

I would like to thank David Chamberlain and Janet Cubey for comments on the text.
I would also like to thank the Stanley Smith Horticultural Trust for a grant allowing me to make the March/April 1997 trip.

KEITH RUSHFORTH *is a member of the Group and is a Chartered Forester and Arboricultural Consultant. He has led several botanical expeditions to Bhutan, China, Tibet and Vietnam*

CAMELLIA SASANQUA

LOGAN EDGAR

In the past almost all autumn or winter flowering camellias have been known or listed under the name *C. sasanqua*. In fact, apart from the true sasanquas, several other equally distinct species have been included, chief among these being *C. hiemalis* and *C. vernalis*. More recently, other species giving rise to small leaved, early flowering plants have been interbred. In particular *C. lutchuensis* has been bred in to give us its superb scent, supreme in the case of *C.* 'Quintessence', to my mind the finest scented camellia to date, and *C.* 'Scentuous', a good runner up, as well as several others. So, in order to simplify an otherwise complex group, we include all these similar early flowering, and mostly scented camellias under the umbrella name of *C. sasanqua*.

With such a variety of beautiful plants available and flowering at a time of year when little else flowers (October-December) it is a puzzle to understand why this group has been so widely ignored in the United Kingdom. The reasons are probably twofold. First, sasanquas have been little known and grossly ignored by garden writers and the gardening public, and secondly, because nurseries have done little to show the public their true worth. After all, why should anyone in his right state of mind bother to display an exhibition stand of sasanquas at the worst time of year, when, by waiting two or three months, he can put on a dazzling display of *C. japonica, C. reticulata,* or hybrids.

In fact, sasanquas are not difficult to grow. They are generally just as hardy as japonicas and hybrids. There are always exceptions in each group. They tolerate more alkaline conditions than japonicas or hybrid camellias, and certainly require less feeding. Here, however, a note of warning must be sounded in these respects :

(1) In my experience, young plants require more protection against a freezing winter spell than most young japonicas or hybrids.

(2) In order to set flower buds in any reasonable number, sasanquas require more heat and warmth than japonicas and hybrids, and

(3) One must bear in mind that a group of plants which flower in October, November and December, are bound to be exposed to spells of atrocious weather. This will ruin their flowering display and therefore preventative steps must be taken. In this respect, sasanquas are no different from dozens of other late autumn or winter flowering plants. Clearly if they can be given the protection of a greenhouse, conservatory or even a porch at flowering time, the owners will be well rewarded by seeing their blooms at their best, unmarred by the weather and scenting the air (for almost all sasanquas, unlike japonicas and hybrids, are scented).

In addition, their scent emerges best in indoor conditions. These are obviously the best conditions we can give our sasanquas, and with so many more greenhouses or conservatories now being included in modern garden design and architecture, this should, for many, present no problem. However, do not despair if you can provide neither of these. How about a south-facing wall or garage wall, or even a west or south-east wall? If there is no house wall available, then you should locate the sunniest and most sheltered spot in the garden for your plants.

Perhaps a word should now be said about planting, growing and propagating sasanquas. So far as soil conditions are concerned, they are not greatly different from other camellias, although, as already mentioned, they will tolerate a somewhat more alkaline soil and very certainly resent any form of over feeding.

At this stage it might be useful to set out the way that we propagate and grow on sasanquas at Coghurst Nursery. Orthodox cuttings (about four leaves of semi-ripe seasons growth) are taken at any time from about July to December. Cuttings are taken immediately above or below a node and that leaf is cut off reducing the cutting (if possible) to three leaves. The usual 1.5-2cm (½-¾in) sliver of bark is removed from one side near the base and the prepared cuttings are dipped in rooting powder and inserted in standard seed trays in a mix of 50 per cent moss peat and 50 per cent fine cambark, and placed in a normal propagating frame (basal heating by electric cables and plastic close over the propagating bed). No fertilizer is included in the mix. We have found such an addition to be lethal. When well rooted, cuttings are hardened off and potted up into 9cm (3½in) pots in fibrous Bulrush peat. No doubt other similar peats would be equally satisfactory but whatever is used it must be moss peat and coarse fibrous grade. We find that even at this stage no fertilizer should be added. If it is, we find we suffer very high and totally unacceptable losses. Once the cuttings are well established, we give an occasional liquid feed of a weak solution of Phostrogen for acid-loving plants. This seems to be all the young sasanquas require for quite a long time.

We find that sasanquas grow extremely slowly so they are not repotted until the following year when, to save time, they go into 1, 1½ or 2 litre pots according to the cultivar's speed of growth. Throughout, fertilizer is kept to a bare minimum. From that point growing on to point of sale (or planting into the open ground or the conservatory for the amateur gardener) will take another one or two seasons. Once established in the open ground, or larger containers in the greenhouse, we find an occasional feed with Phostrogen to be adequate.

Finally, it may be worthwhile to select several outstanding plants from the dozens available (always an invidious task). At Coghurst Nursery we currently grow some 30 different cultivars. Ignoring for a moment the wonderful Australian 'Paradise' sasanquas bred and introduced by Bob Cherry, among our favourites would be the scented singles, 'Oleifera', 'Narumigata', (very similar and both white touched with an edge of pink when opening), 'Plantation Pink', a fine, large, scented single pink; 'Lucinda', a large semi-double to peony form scented pink; 'Mine No Yuki', a semi-double white; 'Kanjiro', a large semi-double deep rose, shading to red at the petal margins, and 'Jean May', a semi-double to double, shell pink.

To conclude, there must be a brief word about the 'Paradise' strain of sasanquas, although there is a fuller account of these in the article that follows by Bob Cherry, the man who hybridized, grew, selected and introduced them. At Coghurst we are, as far as I know, the only retail nursery in the UK which has grown and supplied them to the gardening public since their introduction three or four years ago. We can only say this – that they are superb. The flower form, size, colour and perfume are quite outstanding. We have grown and propagated them for several seasons now and find them no more difficult than the older sasanquas. In many respects, they are easier. They certainly do not seem to miss their Australian sun too badly, for grown (and wintered) in a shade structure, they have budded up profusely.

The one thing we cannot say for certain is whether they are hardy planted outside in one of our bad winters. First indications are encouraging, but with plants that we have had for only three or four years, it is too early to say. However, looking at it rationally, who in his right mind would plant outdoors a gorgeous scented, say white tinged pink flowered shrub, the blooms the size of any of our japonicas and hybrids, and expect to see it at its best in November, December or January, in a typical British winter. I know of no other flower where such a risk would be taken. While orders of preference are always a matter of personal taste, I think it is fair to say that, from the experience of our limited years of growing the 'Paradise' strain, we would select 'Venessa', 'Blush', ' Hilda' and 'Belinda', in that order, for floriferousness, scent and ease of growing.

May the 'Paradise' strain, already wonderfully varied, progress from strength to strength and may they, together with our older sasanquas, for so long ignored, be recognised for their true worth, and given the support by garden writers, planners and gardeners which they so truly deserve.

LOGAN EDGAR *is a member of the Group, a partner in Coghurst Nursery, Hastings and author of* Camellias: the Complete Guide

THE SASANQUAS FROM PARADISE

BOB CHERRY

In the UK autumn-flowering camellias, other than a few cultivars available from specialist nurseries, have been sadly under promoted. Few if any introductions of the last 50 years have been offered for sale. Little has been written by the gardening press, there is scant reference to sasanquas in gardening books, and generally there is a reluctance by gardeners to try something new, or by garden centres to stock something new. Little wonder then that *C. sasanqua* cultivars are all too rarely seen in this country.

In Australia, by contrast, *C. sasanqua* is the most popular garden camellia, outselling japonicas and hybrids. They are much prized as hedging, and also for their sun tolerance and speed of growth. With their early autumn flowering they extend the flowering season in a camellia enthusiast's garden by three months.

The 'Paradise' range of sasanquas has recently been introduced into the UK. These were originally raised at Paradise Plants, my nursery situated in the hills to the north of Sydney, on the east coast of Australia. As a nurseryman I much admired *C. sasanqua* and when I started the garden at 'Paradise' I planted them in drifts. For to my way of thinking *C. sasanqua* is to the Sydney landscape what the rhododendrons can be, that

is to say, drifts of colour, in the UK. A limited range of cultivars was available, and so I decided to do my own crossing. However every time I made a deliberate cross, I found seed would not set, due to rain, the activity of birds or some other mishap. Consequently, instead, I collected open pollinated seed from each variety and grew about 2,000 seedlings each year.

When the first seedlings flowered I soon learnt which trees produced the best seedlings. 'Plantation Pink' produced offspring similar to the parent; 'Violet Weymouth' produced seedlings that sprawled, and 'Red Willow' willowy offspring. The best parents were 'Jane Morgan', 'Showae No Sakae', 'Jennifer Susan' and 'Sparkling Burgundy'. Over a period of 10 or 12 years over 20,000 seedlings were grown. A few hundred of the best were planted out, and from these about 30 were selected for growing on and marketing.

In the favourable climate of Sydney camellias flower within three years of sowing seed. Seed set on plants is very heavy, so that growing large numbers of seedlings is not the trouble it can be in cooler climates. This is the main reason that Australia and New Zealand produce many new cultivars of plants each year.

Cultivars of the Paradise strain that are so far available are:

'Paradise Sayaka' (Plant Breeders Rights [PBR] to be applied for)

It is an attractive single to semi-double with a pure simple form. Flowers are white and broadly edged with a soft salmon-pink border, making it both attractive and distinctive. 'Paradise Sayaka' is early flowering and flowers over a long period. Plant habit is upright and dense with attractive, long dark green leaves. Suitable for sun or shade, its upright habit makes it ideal for specimen planting, tub culture or screens (to 4m), where a narrow growing cultivar is desired.

'Paradise Joan' (PBR to be applied for)

It produces extra showy, large, red, loose informal double flowers interspersed with attractive golden stamens. Plants are upright and vigorous with an open habit initially, but maturing to a more dense habit. 'Paradise Joan' is one of the earliest of the sasanquas to flower and does so over a very long period. It is ideal for growing as an espalier.

'Paradise Audrey'

Dense upright grower to 3m (10ft), producing delightful pale shell pink, informal double flowers. Early to flower and flowers are produced over a long season. Suitable for hedges or screens or as a tub or garden specimen. It will grow in sun or shade.

'Paradise Helen'

This free flowering sasanqua has an elegant upright growth habit. Masses of brilliant pink buds open to dazzling white with a delicate soft pink shading. Flowers are large informal double with petaloid stamens. Early flowering, quick growing and very floriferous, it is ideal for hedges or screens, or as a tub or garden specimen. Suitable for sun or shade.

'Paradise Belinda'

A compact grower with dark green glossy foliage with very large flowers for a sasanqua (up to 13cm/5in across). They are semi-double, with a central mix of stamens and petaloid stamens. The colour is a deep rose. Belinda's compact habit makes it ideal for tub culture.

'Paradise Venessa'

This is the fastest growing of the Paradise range. It has large, full, informal double flowers white flushed pink on petal margins, and fragrant. Its upright vigorous habit makes it ideal for hedging.

'Paradise Glow'

A seedling of 'Plantation Pink'. The flowers are large single and bright pink. It has lovely golden central stamens. Its vigorous upright growth makes it useful as an espalier.

'Paradise Pearl'

A bushy, upright, compact grower with glossy shiny leaves. The flowers are white flushed pink, large double to semi-double. The opening flowers are formal, and semi-double when fully opened. Ideal for tubs and hedging and useful for espalier work.

'Paradise Blush'

It has compact, slender, upright growth and small flowers. Bright red buds open to dazzling pure white star-shaped flowers.

'Paradise Hilda'

It has vigorous upright growth habit, with flowers full informal double and a deep rosy pink. It is suitable for pots, hedging and espalier.

'Paradise Gillian'

Upright slender growth. The flowers are large white with each petal delicately edged soft pink. The opening flowers are formal in form, and when fully opened, semi-double.

'Paradise Barbara'

This is a compact, dense, bushy plant with very dark green leaves, that contrast with the pure white and large single flowers. This is the best hedging sasanqua of them all.

THE PARADISE DWARFS

These dwarf sasanquas are unique in having small leaves and a compact habit, making them ideal to plant where a low hedge is required. In Australia they are quite often planted instead of box. They have the advantage over box of quicker growth and for three months of the year, masses of flower. These Dwarfs make ideal tub specimens and lend themselves also to topiary work. Ideal also as standards, they open up new dimensions to camellia culture, and are perfect for conservatories. They are as follows.

'Paradise Petite'

This is a delightful small-leafed sasanqua, compact and dense in habit, with medium-sized, informal double flowers of a bright pink shade.

'Paradise Little Liane'

This has a compact dwarf habit with small shining dark green leaves, and medium double flowers white flushed soft pink.

'Paradise Baby Jane'

This is the most compact of all, growing only 8cm (3in) a year, and with a very dense compact habit. The flowers are small, semi-double, white edged bright pink. This cultivar is ideal for tubs and window boxes (see fig. 9).

It is my intention that over the next few years further new cultivars will be added to complement the range.

BOB CHERRY *is the owner of Paradise Plants, Kulnura, NSW, Australia*

RAISED IN NEW ZEALAND

VONNIE CAVE

Since 1960 camellia enthusiasts in New Zealand have raised over 380 new cultivars. Until about 1975 the greatest number of new registrations came within the Reticulata hybrid group as the Yunnan Reticulatas had arrived in New Zealand and members of the New Zealand Camellia Society were quick to realise that these plants grew well in most parts of New Zealand, flowered profusely and set seed readily.

Meantime a slower steady trickle of *C. japonica* were coming through and the raising of what we call the 'non-reticulata hybrids' gained impetus and this trend has continued to the present day. Some growers began using *C. saluenensis* with *C. reticulata* and *C. japonica*, while others experimented with *C. pitardii* and some of the progeny from those first crosses are still regarded as very good camellias after 35 years. The group of non-reticulata hybrids on the New Zealand register is now much the biggest list on our files. Gradually other species of camellias have been introduced to New Zealand and crosses with or chance seedlings from species such as *C. fraterna*, *C. lutchuensis*, *C. rosiflora*, *C. transnokoensis* and *C. tsaii* have all been tried. In using such small flowered species a range of multi-flowered hybrids have appeared with miniature flowers. Some have attractive growth habits and foliage and it is important that the foliage is small to remain in proportion with the size of the flowers.

Let us look at some of the first camellias registered in New Zealand, those by Dr Brian Doak. Number one on the list is 'Phyl Doak', named for his wife. It was a *C. saluenensis* × *C. reticulata* 'Capt. Rawes' and is still grown. Others he registered from similar crosses were 'Fair Lass', 'Brian' and 'Barbara Clark' and all these are still about in older gardens, 'Brian' being suitable for a large hedgerow.

Of the many reticulatas registered Jack Clark raised a big proportion of the first ones and of the ones I have growing, 'Rhonda Kerri' and 'Eden Queen' are still very good camellias, 'Rhonda Kerri' for such a great early display and 'Eden Queen' for high quality red blooms later.

Other good red reticulatas that have held their place are 'Glowing Embers' from Harry Burwell and 'Margaret Hilford' registered by Jim Rolfe, the latter often showing up as a winner in camellia shows.

With 53 registrations to his credit and many of those plants featuring in camellia collections throughout the country, the name of Les Jury will be long remembered in the camellia world. 'Elegant Beauty', a *C. saluenensis* × *C. japonica* 'Elegans' is a great garden plant that can be kept along a trellis or wall to good effect. 'Debbie' and

'Senorita' have also stood the test of time and 'Ballet Queen', 'Daintiness' and 'Anticipation' are all excellent in the garden.

'Elsie Jury', named for Les's first wife, has been very successful in the USA as a show bloom. It was the result of a cross between *C. saluensis* and *C. japonica* 'Pukekura', a white seedling from the New Plymouth area. The next registration, named after Les's second wife, was for 'Mona Jury', which came from crossing a hybrid with *C. japonica* 'Betty Sheffield'. It seems subject to damage before fully opening as the petals are exposed, but undamaged, is a beautiful bloom. 'Jubilation' is from a similar cross and the plant has a very open style of growth.

In 1991, a nursery which acquired Les's plants after his death, registered a red camellia in his name, 'Les Jury'. A plant with spreading growth and smallish white flowers called 'Avalanche' is another of those registered after his death, and it could be useful as a ground cover plant. A small formal to peony-flowered camellia – about 8cm (3in) – with very unusual red to purple colouring has also been registered and is called 'Sir Victor Davies' after the founder of the nursery. Japonicas 'Fuyajo' and 'Zambo' were the parents of this camellia.

Jim Finlay is a very enthusiastic grower who has been working for many years on improving the fragrance of camellia blooms. He has introduced a number; one of the earlier ones 'High Fragrance' came about from a cross between 'Bertha Harms' and a hybrid and is pale ivory pink about 10cm(4in) and with good fragrance. 'Scentuous' with 7cm(2½in) white flushed pink fragrant blooms flowers very freely, and a newer reg-istration, 'Sweet Emma', is a medium to large bloom, of anemone form with white centre, the outer petals blushed pink and a very appealing spicy fragrance. Jim Finlay has registered several red-flowered blooms with fragrance, mainly with 'Kramer's Supreme' as a parent. Among these are 'Yummy Fragrance', 'Prime Fragrance', 'Jim Finlay's Fragrant', 'Scented Fireglow', 'Sentimental', and 'Scentasia'. 'Tony Finlay's Fragrant' is a pink anenome form and 'Fragrant Lady' is semi-double, ivory white with a pink flush on the outside petals, and both share 'Mrs Bertha Harms' as a parent.

Mrs Bettie Durrant was instrumental in using *C. pitardii* to produce some of the hybrid camellias she registered and 'Grace Caple' was one of these, the other parent a *C. japonica*. The 12cm (4½in) flower is very pale pink to white, semi-double to peony, and although pale in colouring it seems to stand the weather well in our country. 'Snippet' and 'Prudence' were also *C. pitardii* seedlings and both have soft lavender-pink blooms, about 8-9cm (3-3½in) and are compact growers. 'Snippet' seems to be grown more than 'Prudence' – possibly it blooms more freely and the flower is of slightly better texture.

Perhaps Bettie's best known introduction is 'Nicky Crisp' which was named for her grandson and raised from a *C. pitardii* × *C. pitardii*. The plant is of slow compact growth, flowering prolifically with soft pink blooms of about 8-10cm (3-4in). The blooms look attractive on the plant in the garden and on the show bench; the semi-double flowers look fresh and clean, the inner bases of the petals with almost a lime green tinge of colour.

For those who prefer a dwarf plant, Neville Haydon's 'Baby Bear' is ideal. The soft pink 2cm (¾in) single blooms are produced profusely and drop whole when mature. 'Baby Bear' was the result of a cross between *C. rosiflora* and *C. tsaii* and a second registration was made from the cross, the cultivar called 'Baby Willow'. This plant is also dwarf but has a weeping habit and small 1.5cm (½in) single white flowers.

A new registration from Neville is for 'Seaspray', a single white 4cm (1½in) bloom with golden stamens which appears mid to late in the season. It comes from a seedling of 'Snowdrop', one of Edgar Sebire's Australian raised camellias of the multi-flowered type. 'Peekaboo' is also a newish one from the Haydon nursery, Camellia Haven. It is a bright pink formal double, 7.5cm (3in) which flowers mid season to late and is a seedling of 'Fairy Boquet', which also originated from the Sebire nursery.

'Noni Haydon', a *C. pitardii* × *C. pitardii* was also raised by Neville and named after his mother. The flowers are full peony, about 13cm (5in) and bloom early in the season. They are deepish pink when fresh tending to fade a little as they age. 'Sunsong' is another hybrid of his, this one a pink formal double of about 10cm (4in) from a seed of 'Elegant Beauty'.

'Takanini' (see fig. 10) is the name of a 'Mark Alan' japonica seedling that Neville raised, naming it for the area where his nursery is situated near Auckland. This is one of the most interesting of all the recent introductions in New Zealand as the plant starts opening a few blooms in February and March, before even the sasanquas have started, and carries on blooming all season,

until October and November. It seems to have the ability to go on setting buds over the winter months when most camellias show a certain number at the beginning of the flowering season and that is it. 'Takanini' does not appear to have a huge number of buds at any time, but more seem to form throughout the flowering season in my area. The anemone form flowers are a deep wine red, about 8.5cm (3½in) and when the weather is cold the colour changes from wine red to a bluish purple. They appear to stand the weather quite well too.

Neville also registered 'Volcano', ('San Dimas' × 'Mark Alan') and this is a high anemone form of scarlet red colouring, the flowers about 11cm (4½in) in diameter.

'Harry Cave' was the name given to this 'Bob Hope' seedling raised by Harry and registered in 1989 shortly after he passed away. The pollen is bright yellow and the semi-double flowers with shiny petals a cherry red, about 8-9cm (3-3½in) across on a slow growing compact plant. An excellent garden plant.

Three interesting dark reds were raised by the late Trevor Lennard. The one I have is 'Nick Carter', a 'Fuyajo' seedling registered in 1991 with light white tipped petaloids and golden stamens in the anemone centre of an 8cm (3in) bloom. The plant seems slow growing to date. 'Alisha Carter', another from the same parentage, is a 7cm (2½in) peony form and of the same dark black-red colouring, while 'Liz Carter' is also dark red, an 8cm (3in) semi-double and is a chance seedling. Weather damage is not as evident on dark blooms as on the paler flowers so these cultivars could be well worth trying in England, providing of course, that

C. japonica does well in the area.

Felix Jury, brother of Les, has raised some excellent camellias, apart from magnolias, nerines, celmisias and many other genera. 'Waterlily', a *C. saluenensis* × *C. japonica* 'K. Sawada' came through in 1966 and has been a popular hybrid of upright growth. Some of the formal blooms open in my garden early in the season, shutting down over the colder months to open again late in the camellia season. 'Dreamboat' is from the same cross and produces similar lavender-pink coloured formal flowers, but most of those on 'Dreamboat' have an incurving petal edge which gives a very different effect. In camellia shows a good 'Dreamboat' is hard to beat in the non-reticulata hybrid classes. Other formal blooms registered by Felix Jury include 'Softly', a very pale pink *C. saluenensis* × *C. japonica* 'Joshua Youtz' of about 10cm (4in) and 'Julie Felix' from the same cross, a deeper pink and slightly larger to about 13cm (4in). 'Mimosa Jury' was named for his wife, also a keen gardener, and it is also a formal double pale pink bloom from the same cross.

'Rose Boquet' is a heavy rose form to peony flower, of mid pink and about 12cm (4½in), again a cross from *C. saluenensis* but this time with *C. japonica* 'Tiffany'. In good weather the blooms are beautiful, but rough conditions can mark them and really hot sun tends to fade them. The dwarf form of 'Itty Bit' has made this cultivar very popular and strangely it was the result of crossing two upright growers, *C. saluenensis* and *C. japonica* 'Debutante'. The small 6cm (2½in) pale lavender-pink anemone flowers are borne in profusion making this a very useful garden plant of low spreading habit.

Felix Jury's son Mark is carrying on his parent's interests in plants and has registered a camellia called 'Fairy Blush'. This is also one of the multi-flowered and small-leaved camellias which are creating a lot of interest nowadays. It is an upright grower, the buds are deep pink on the outside opening to look like apple blossoms of about 5cm (2in). The seedling was from the species *C. lutchuensis*.

Os Blumhardt is another New Zealand grower who dabbles with many different kinds of plants, but his camellia hybridizing has brought forth some distinctive camellias. 'Dreamy Baby', although only 6cm (2½in) has a little reticulata in its mixed background. The mid-pink flowers come very early and show gold stamens in the semi-double flowers. 'Gay Baby' is a mass bloomer with 5cm (2in) flowers of deep orchid pink while 'Fairy Wand' from the same 'Ruby Bells' × 'Tiny Princess' background is also a spectacular mass of 4cm (1½in) flowers of bright rose red.

The smallest flower of Os Blumhardt's crosses is called 'Tiny Star' and it is soft pink with firm little semi-double flowers resembling flowers made of icing sugar. They measure 2-5cm (¾-2in) and look most attractive on my plant which is trimmed back against a wall. Flowering time is early to mid-season. 'Tiny Princess' and 'Berenice Boddy' are the parents of this mini miniature.

'Sugar Dream' with deep pink guard petals and a bunch of cream petaloids in the centre of the 8cm (3in) flower is one of the outstanding inter-species crosses and when this cultivar blooms very early in the season it is really appreciated. The flowers don't hold for long but are really enjoyed while at their best. The *C. sasanqua* × *C. reticulata*

Fig. 1 (above): R. ciliatum × R. edgeworthii *'Best'. A new scented hybrid for indoors or outside (see p.13). Fig. 2 (below):* R. liliiflorum. *A later flowering and recently introduced Maddenia species with a lily habit for growing indoors (see p.14)*

Fig. 3 (above left): Zhang Wen, the interpreter, and the 'floral feast' above Napa-Hai, nr Zhongdian, Yunnan (see p.20). Fig. 4 (above right): Azalea mortieriana, Vershcaffelt's first 12 hybrids; the litho in the Annales of 1846 (see p.30). Fig. 5 (below): BNNZ 1997 Yunnan expedition camp below the Doker La, on the Mekong-Salween divide (see p.24)

Fig. 6 (above): R. lanatoides *flowering on the Tra La, in the Rong Chu Valley, SE Tibet (see p.17). Fig. 7 (left):* R. aff. delavayi *in flower on Suoi Doi, in the north of Vietnam (see p.37). Fig. 8 (below):* R. tanastylum *on the Fan Si Pan, in the north of Vietnam (see p.36)*

Fig. 9 (left): Camellia *'Paradise Baby Jane'* one of the range of *'Paradise Dwarfs'* (see p.44).
Fig. 10 (below): Camellia japonica *'Takanini'*, a seedling with a long flowering season, raised by Neville Haydon, nr Auckland, New Zealand (see p.47)

Fig. 11 (left): R. cinnabarinum *Concatenans Group at Lingholm Gardens, Cumbria - winner of the Photographic Competition. Fig. 12 (above right):* R. falconeri *hybrid at Clyne Castle Garden Swansea, a runner up in the Photographic Competition. Fig. 13 (below):* R. 'Betty Wormald' *another Photographic Competition runner up.*

Fig. 14 (above): Magnolia campbellii *var.* mollicomata *'Peter Borlase', one of the three 'stars' of Lanhydrock, Cornwall (see p.51). Fig. 15 (below left):* Magnolia × soulangeana *'Alba Superba' at Bodnant Garden, N Wales, another runner up in the Photographic Competition (see p.66). Fig. 16 (right): A 600-year-old* Pinus bungeana *(the lace-bark pine), Seoul, S Korea, photographed during the 1997 Magnolia Society tour (see p.59)*

Fig.17 (above): Jim Gardiner, Curator of the RHS Garden, Wisley, and Magnolia 'Spectrum' at the Chollipo Arboretum, S Korea (p.59). Fig. 18 (left): Magnolia 'Vulcan' see (p.65). Fig. 19 (below): R. 'Russellianum Southamptonia' (see p.63)

Fig. 20 (above):An earlier than usual bloom of R. hodgsonii *shown in March 1997 at the Early Rhododendron Competition (see p.72)*

Fig. 21 (left): an impressive display of 12 camellia blooms which won the Leonardslee Bowl for Mrs Ann Hooton of Loxwood, W Sussex (see p.78)

hybrid 'Dream Girl' was one of the parents and *C. oliefera* 'Jaune' the other, the offspring showing the petal colour of one and the petaloids of the other.

A 1984 registration from Os Blumhardt was for 'Black Opal', a very dark black-red flower colour with contrasting gold stamens, this one bred from 'Ruby Bells' and 'Kurotsubaki'. The plant is compact and slow growing and the semi-double 6-8cm (2½-3in) flowers come mid-to-late in the season. The new growth on this plant is quite red in colour, but the plant Os Blumhardt registered as 'Night Rider' from the same cross is a more vigorous upright grower that produces more of this spectacular red new growth each season. 'Night Rider's flowers are also a very dark black-red and are about 7cm (2½in) diameter and semi-double in form. One of my plants of this is kept against a wall, pruned flattish but not espaliered, and the late season flowers followed by the display of new growth are very worth while. Grown in the open 'Night Rider' becomes quite a dense upright plant.

These are just some of the New Zealand raised camellias that I happen to have grown, seen, read or heard about and no doubt there are many more. With a lot of the housing in the suburban areas of our country being built on smaller sections there appears to be a need for smaller shrubs and a number of these small and multi-flowered camellias seem to be in demand, although they won't all stay as small shrubs. It is hard to convince some of the public here that a plant with miniature flowers is not a miniature grower. Those raised from the small-flowered Chinese species could perhaps be easier to prune and keep than the big strong reticulatas or japonicas, and the plants look daintier than the heavy dark-foliaged japonicas.

It is impossible for me to say that any particular ones of those mentioned will thrive in UK conditions, but possibly some indication could be taken from their parentage and your knowledge of which species do well in your area.

VONNIE CAVE *lives at Wanganui, New Zealand, and is a Director of the International Camellia Society*

THE THREE 'STAR MAGNOLIAS' OF LANHYDROCK

PETER BORLASE

Of all the National Trust Gardens in Cornwall, Lanhydrock is probably the least favoured climatically. It faces north-east on a hillside overlooking the valley of the River Fowey, about 14.5km (9 miles) from the coast, which reduces the maritime influence, and the south-west corner of Bodmin Moor is only some 6.5km (4 miles) away. Late frosts can spoil a wonderful display of early flower. The garden extends to about 12ha (30 acres) and surrounds Lanydrock House on three sides with formal and informal areas and with woodland areas beyond the formal garden. The soil is a good rich loam with a pH of around 5.0.

We have no confirming record but, on the north wall of the house, the ancient *M. grandiflora*, a species introduced to Britain from the SE United States in the early 18th century, must be among the first plantings of magnolias at Lanhydrock House. The house was built between 1630 and 1650.

I was fortunate enough to be appointed Head Gardener at Lanhydrock in 1966 and I like to think I am largely responsible for magnolias now forming a major part of the informal and woodland sections of the garden. A few records were passed to me by my predecessor Mr G A Potter who was Head Gardener for over 30 years from 1933 to 1965. During his first year he well remembered planting five magnolias, comprising three *M. campbellii* subsp *mollicomata* and two *M. × veitchii* (*M. campbellii × M. denudata*) all purchased from Veitch's Nurseries of Exeter. In 1953 the property was given to the National Trust by the 7th Viscount Clifden, who was a batchelor. He died seven years later in 1966, the year also in which Mr Potter retired. By this time there were still only a few magnolias in place. The earlier plantings had grown prolifically, attaining some 15m (50ft) in just 30 years, and it was clear to me that magnolias would do very well at Lanhydrock. As a result I decided to build on these original plantings and add some more of the outstanding species and cultivars. The garden now contains no fewer than 130 different magnolias. One of my dreams was always to go on a plant hunting expedition to seek magnolias in the wild but it was never realised, and it occurred to me that the next best thing would be to raise plants from garden seed.

In 1970 Michael Taylor, Head Gardener at Trewithen Garden at Probus, also in Cornwall, created by the late G H Johnstone OBE VMH, raised three seedlings from seed collected from the tree of *M. cylindrica* at Trewithen. One of these seedlings was given to me as a small 25cm (10in) plant by the late Mrs Alison Johnstone in 1974. I planted it in the lower part of the informal garden at Lanhydrock when it was some 75-90cm (2½-3ft) tall and multi stemmed. I later reduced the plant to a single stem as it showed an inclination to develop as a tree rather than a shrub. As it happened this seedling was ultimately the only one of the three raised by Michael Taylor to survive. It first flowered in 1981 at 11 years of age and after 14 years it was approximately 6m (20ft) tall. It was while discussing this seedling with my friend Mr Nigel Holman of Chyverton Garden and looking more closely into the structure of the flowers that it was decided to seek the help of the Royal Botanic Gardens, Kew, to ascertain the probable parentage. Their consultant taxonomist, Michael Lear, took material to Kew and considered it with Christopher Grey-Wilson, and it was recognized as something very special.

Kew decided to give this fine hybrid the name of 'Albatross', a name that somehow reflects the nature of the very large white flowers which appear to float on its branches. Nine broadly ovate tepals some 8-10cm (3-4in) wide make up an impressive flower, up to 25cm (10in) in diameter. A visiting American member of the Magnolia Society in 1987 seeing the tree in full bloom was seen to doff his hat first in homage to a magnificent tree.

M. × *veitchii* 'Peter Veitch' which was growing near the specimen of *M. cylindrica* from which the seeds were collected is assumed to be the pollen parent, from which the plant appears to have inherited looks, flower size, and number of tepals. 'Albatross' was named in 1985 and registered in 1992 (No 18769) with Dorothy J Callaway, the

Registrar of the Magnolia Society. Dried specimens, flowers and leaves, are in the Herbarium at Kew. It was awarded an FCC in 1996.

The second Lanhydrock 'star', *M. sprengeri* 'Lanhydrock', was also a seedling originating at Trewithen. This turned out to be a deeper and more striking colour than its *M. sprengeri* parent.

I have already explained that at Lanhydrock frost can often spoil a beautiful display of flower, and so I decided to extend the magnolia plantings further into the higher garden from where cold air drains away more freely and reduces the incidence of frost damage. To a certain extent this has succeeded. As a result *M. sprengeri* 'Lanhydrock' has a fairly prominent position and when in flower can be seen from many parts of the garden. As one walks through the Park the mass of rich pink is quite breathtaking against the the dark background of the hillside. Closer inspection of the very deep pink flowers shows that they are at first cup shaped, eventually opening to the horizontal and reaching some 20cm (8in) or more across. The leaves are ovate and 20-25cm (8-10in) long. *M.* 'Lanhydrock' was planted in 1969 as a five-year-old seedling, and the first flowers appeared in 1980. As it has matured it has become one of the most spectacular magnolias in the garden and among the most richly coloured of all cultivars.

The third star is *M. mollicomata* 'Peter Borlase' (see fig. 14), and has much more of a personal touch. It was raised in 1967 from natural open-pollinated seed. From some 80 to 100 seedlings I selected 10 which for various reasons looked good strong specimens with well developed and well shaped foliage.

The remainder of the batch of seedlings was used by a local nursery for grafting under-stocks. The 10 seedlings were grown on in our nursery until large enough to be planted out and in view of the fact that they were just untried seedlings, I had them planted along the west perimeter of the garden to determine their wind hardiness. I can say they have proved to be no problem and have stood up perfectly well to our prevailing winds.

In the spring of 1985 several of these seedlings started to flower at 18 years of age. Most were what one would call pale magnolia pink, typical of *M. mollicomata*. However nature had smiled on us just once. One seedling was quite different and a real one-off special. It was a most unusual deep reddish rose pink with a pale bar through the centre of the tepal. All the seed came from the same specimen of *M. mollicomata* which was planted after the Second World War in 1949/50. The origin of this tree remains obscure, as for some reason, Viscount Clifden did not pass on this information to Mr Potter, and in those days Head Gardeners were not encouraged to keep a detailed diary of plantings, as we do now. It is possible that the pollen parent could be *M. sargentiana* var. *robusta* which stands next to the seed parent. The flower is perhaps not as large as some mollicomata cultivars with a diameter of 15-20cm (6-8in). The tepals are broad and rounded, the leaves are almost obovate 15-23cm (6-9in) long which is typical. A tall well-shaped tree, in common with many magnolias it does have a tendancy to flower biennially.

All three Lanhydrock 'stars' can hold their own for beauty and hardiness in any magnolia company. Before I retired I made propagating material available and plants are now growing in collections both here in the United Kingdom and, where the climate is suitable, overseas. In the UK they promise to be good garden plants for general use and, like most magnolias, seem to do well in any situation that gives them a reasonable degree of protection from untimely frosts.

PETER BORLASE *lives in Bodmin, Cornwall, and until his retirement was Head Gardener at the National Trust Garden Lanhydrock, near Bodmin*

MAGNOLIAS FROM SEED

MAURICE FOSTER

There are few who have either the vision or the devotion to plant only for their grandchildren. One of the major deterrents to growing magnolias from seed is the widespread but erroneous belief that seedlings require at least a generation and possibly two to produce a flower. It is true that *M. campbellii* and *M. campbellii* subsp. *mollicomata* may take over 20 years to do so and extraordinary stories from Cornwall cite examples of over 30 years for the former species – and one species can tend to give the genus as a whole a bad name. Apart from the fact that the sunnier and more rigorous climate away from the gulf stream seaboard could possibly shorten adolescence with better summer ripening of the wood (M Charles Raffil – *M. campbellii* × *M. mollicomata* – required only 11 or 12 years to achieve florescence in the home counties) there are many other species and their hybrids that require significantly less patient forbearance. In the climate of west Kent it has only taken some five or six years for flowers to develop on a varied range of seedlings. Some examples – *M. cylindrica* seed sown 29 December 1986, planted 8 April 1989, flower 6 April 1992; 'Lennei' × *M. sprengeri diva*: seed sown 11 April 1988, planted 21 March 1990, flower 16 April 1993; 'Dark Shadow' (Gresham) × *M. mollicomata*: seed sown 9 April 1991, planted 23 May 1993, flower 11 April 1997. The late spring/early summer flowering group of the Oyama section will also flower within five years or so. These times are not unconscionably long and are about the same as or even shorter than for many rhododendrons or indeed other woody genera.

A further deterrent is a belief that open pollinated or hybrid seed will yield mostly mediocre results that will be highly unlikely to differ substantially from or improve on what has gone before. Sowing this type of seed is therefore not worthwhile. This may indeed be true of *M.* × *soulangeana* forms where expectations of something better are not high; but elsewhere in this issue Peter Borlase describes three outstanding Cornish magnolias in the garden at Lanhydrock which apart from their beauty – in flower they can hold the stage with any new US or New Zealand hybrid – share another interesting characteristic. They were each raised from natural open-pollinated seed, collected in Cornish gardens. There are other examples: *M.* 'Harold Hillier', a late white of exceptional size and substance which originated at Chyverton, grew from an understock after failure of a graft. The understock, now arguably one of the best whites yet registered, had previously been grown from Caerhays seed.

Thus while it may be thought to be advisable to avoid *M. campbellii* if you are about to apply for a bus pass and *M.* × *soulangeana* on the grounds of unexceptional results there are those who hold that doing the wrong thing and ignoring conventional wisdom is often a good idea. Others believe that there is no such thing as a poor magnolia – only unfavourable comparisons between magnolias in the context of personal preference. It is fair to conclude that results from sowing magnolia seed are always interesting, often excellent and just occasionally worth naming and registering.

Except in the more favoured areas, magnolia seed does not generally set freely in our relatively cold spring conditions, although exceptional crops of seed have been produced in recent years following unseasonably warm spells coinciding with flowering. The failure to ripen a good crop every year may be due to a minimum temperature requirement for pollination; or it may be that the main pollinating agency of tiny beetles, active before the flower fully opens, are either rendered inactive or killed by cold. In the open weather of last March, I recall cutting a large *M. campbellii* flower for the house in the early morning after a ground frost. The flower was unaffected by the cold but scores of dead or comatose beetles cascaded from it when it was cut.

The early summer-flowering magnolias set seed much more readily in the more favourable conditions then prevailing and *M. wilsonii*, *M. sieboldii*, *M. sinensis*, *M. hypoleuca* and *M. globosa* often produce plenty of good fertile seed which germinates readily. Indeed the pink fruit cones of *M. wilsonii* are often sufficiently plentiful to be quite decorative after midsummer.

Magnolia fruits are cone-like structures consisting of irregular clusters of seed cells or follicles, each containing one or possibly two seeds. They are often contorted into grotesque shapes due to the differential development within the cells. These cones become woody as they mature before the follicles split to reveal the bright red or orange seeds within. The process of splitting to actually shedding seed can take up to a month depending on the weather. As soon as the follicles begin to split it is prudent to harvest the cones and allow them to continue to ripen on a dish in a warm, dry environment. After several days it is easy to extract the seeds which are attached to the cone by a very thin silk-like thread. *M. wilsonii* cones can often be seen hanging with red seeds which remain suspended by these threads for a day or so before falling.

The seeds consist of three layers: a brightly coloured red or orange fleshy oily aromatic skin, a hard black stony seed and a thin internal membrane. The outer coat is thought to be attractive to mammals and birds, responsible for dispersal. They are certainly a delicacy for mice from which protection is required in the greenhouse; and in the wild they are frequently riddled with weevils. The coat also prevents the seed from drying out too rapidly, with an eventual loss of viability. One of the cardinal requirements when raising magnolias from seed is never, at any stage, to allow the seed to dry out. Loss of viability is highly probable: some dried seeds may eventually imbibe, develop and germinate up to two years later but most will not.

As well as inhibiting water loss the impermeable outer coat also by definition prevents water uptake and must be removed to begin the process of controlling germination. This is readily achieved by soaking in warm water for as long as it takes to soften the skin. Forty-eight hours is usually enough, and the hard black seed within separates easily, leaving only traces of an oily film on the surface. This is best washed off and an easy practical way is to agitate the seeds with a stiff nailbrush in a kitchen sieve with a mild detergent and finally rinsing them in clean water. The hard seed coat is not waterproof and allows free passage of moisture to and from the embryo. It should be surface dried only and then stored in a way that will maintain a constant moisture level.

As with most woody seeds, germination will only occur after the embryo has matured. The first stage of this process involves a period of chilling to remove built-in dormancy controls. The process is then completed by providing the seed with warmth, when germination will begin quite rapidly. On one occasion seed kept correctly chilled and moist and packeted and mailed from the US has actually developed in the post and arrived with germination beginning and the hard black seed split to reveal the embryo already beginning to push out. The chilling process will of course occur naturally if the seed is sown in the autumn and left for winter cold to do its work. However mice appear to have an exceptional taste for magnolia seeds and, like some other predators will overcome any obstacle to get at them. A crop can be ruined overnight if left outside or in a cold greenhouse. It is therefore best to eliminate this risk and control the moist chilling process. The easiest method is to store the seeds in a polythene bag in the bottom of a domestic refrigerator where the temperature usually ranges from 2-5°C (36-41°F), about the middle of the temperature range 0-6°C (32-43°F) considered to be the most effective in breaking seed dormancy. To maintain moisture at a constant level while maintaining good aeration the seeds must be stored in a suitably moist but not wet medium. A range of material such as damp peat or peat substitute, or sand could be used. A convenient and clean medium is horticultural vermiculite. A handful immersed in water, and then squeezed tightly to remove all excess is ideal. Shaken in with the seeds, and the bag clearly labelled, it takes up little space and simply requires checking every few weeks. When checking it is useful to give the bag a vigorous shake to inhibit stagnation and any build up of moulds. A few pin holes in the bag will also ensure freer passage of air. To break dormancy a cold storage period of 56 days is said to be required though by experiment as little as 42 days has been shown to be enough.

In practice if the seeds are harvested and cleaned in the autumn they may be left in the refrigerator until it is convenient to sow them some 3-5 months later – in winter if artificial warmth can be provided or in spring when temperatures rise. Germination will take place in 3-4 weeks at 16-20°C (61-68°F). It is likely to be even and rapid in the controlled conditions of a greenhouse where temperatures at the upper end of the range can be maintained. Having said this, the prevailing ambient outdoor temperatures in spring will normally produce good germination.

A proportion of the seeds may be sown

conventionally. Others may be kept in the vermiculite bag and simply placed at room temperature and the seeds sown carefully in small individual pots as they split and the radicle shows signs of emerging. While this may be interesting, it is not strictly necessary as magnolias generally will germinate more or less simultaneously; unlike many other woody plants, such as *Sorbus* or *Cotoneaster,* which tend to germinate progressively over a considerable period. In such cases to pre-germinate seeds individually prior to sowing is an obvious advantage, especially if seed is in short supply.

Seeds can be sown in any well aerated, well drained medium. Provided this requirement is met, they will present no special problem. For the amateur producing small batches, a suitable medium is a conventional commercial soilless seed compost mixed 50:50 by volume with vermiculite. Satisfactory and consistent moisture levels are easy to maintain and when the seedlings are transplanted, the light and open compost texture allows easy separation without damage to the delicate roots. Any check to growth is minimal. Seedlings should be transplanted after development of the first true leaves. Though not critical, it is best to transplant them into small liner pots rather than anything bigger. The roots quickly colonize the pots and thereby facilitate a good supply of oxygen to the root system; margins

of safety for watering are improved; and after two months or so the seedlings can be potted on without further disturbance with a compact and well developed root system. By the end of the season, using these procedures and without special facilities seedlings of 30-45cm (1-1½ft) can be achieved, ready for potting on or planting out the following spring after the danger of frost is past.

As indicated earlier, some patience is needed to await the first flowers but many magnolias take no longer than other woody genera to achieve this. Moreover, growing plants is nothing if not creating a keen sense of anticipation, pleasurably feeding the imagination; and the satisfaction of having created something from scratch can be very rewarding, a notion surely shared by the growing number of members applying for magnolia seed through the Group's distribution scheme.

References:

McMillan Browse, P, Notes on the Propagation of Magnolias from Seed, *The Plantsman,* **Vol 8**, Part 1, June 1986

Deno, Professor Norman C, Seed Germination – Theory and Practice, Pennsylvannia State University.

Maurice Foster *is a member of the Group and gardens in Kent. He has been on several expeditions to Bhutan and China*

THE MAGNOLIA SOCIETY ANNUAL MEETING AND TOUR OF SOUTH KOREA

ROBIN HERBERT

The 34th Annual Meeting of the Magnolia Society took place in Seoul on 28 April 1997. The meeting came at the conclusion of a 10-day tour of South Korea that was admirably organised and led by Ferris Miller (Min. Pyong-Gal).

The early part of the tour was designed to introduce those who had never previously visited Korea to the people and their culture. With this objective we were taken to Kyongbokkung Palace in the centre of Seoul. Seoul is a modern cosmopolitan city of 10 million people with four major palaces which are among the few low rise buildings. Because Seoul has been the scene of conflict many times, the Palaces have been subject to substantial restoration. The centrepiece of Kyongbokkung was a substantial traditional edifice with a role that combined the functions of Westminster Hall and Westminster Abbey.

Our next visit was to the National Folk Museum which displayed an excellent tableaux of Korean life from the 5th century onwards. There was a strong emphasis on family authority and discipline, backed up with execution scenes! Those of us of a certain age were delighted to note the veneration paid by children and grandchildren at the 60th birthday of a Korean gentleman.

The first plant that we saw was a superb example of a 600-year-old *Pinus bungeana* (see Fig. 16) in the grounds of one of the city's public buildings. It was held together with metal and wire supports but nevertheless the tree with its flaky white bark was a real show stopper.

On a subsequent day we were taken to two notable collections outside Seoul. The first was to the Department of Forestry Research Centre at Hongnung where there was an arboretum about 40 years old. The trees all had blackened bark due to pollution but we saw good examples of *Acer pseudosieboldianum* and a particularly fine specimen of *Pyrus ussuriensis* var *seoulensis* in bloom.

The second visit was to Kwangnung Arboretum which was approached through nice stands of *Pinus koraiensis* and *Abies holophylla*. The central building contained an exceptional wood museum. Enormous sections of *Zelkova serrata* were on display as well as many artefacts made from wood including a 'Dutch wife' which is a hollow bamboo cylinder which you clasp at night as a substitute for air conditioning! A display of economic botany demonstrated both how *Quercus dentata* leaves are used to wrap up rice and how ground up acorns yield an edible flour.

Before leaving Seoul, our final visit was to Changdokgung Palace. This had large very attractive grounds in which *Pinus densiflora* was the dominant tree, which is the Scots pine of Korea and just as attractive when mature. There were also many examples of *Zelkova serrata*, some over 400 years old and showing signs of stress. The bibliophiles in our party enjoyed the reference to the Palace library as 'the room of fragrant memories'.

The next move, accomplished with a four-hour train journey, was to Kyongju the ancient capital of the Shilla Kingdom in the south-west of Korea. Along with many other tourists we visited three temples in the course of which we saw beautiful drifts of *Rhododendron schlippenbachii*, and good examples of *Quercus variabilis*, *Styrax japonica*, *S. obassia* and *Carpinus cordata*. The last visit of the day was to Sokkulam Buddhist Grotto which dates from the unified Shilla dynasty of the 6th century. UNESCO puts this monument in the same conservation category as the Great Wall of China and we were duly impressed.

The return to the north-west by bus was via Chirisan National Park, which provided a spectacular landscape of narrow valleys in between high mountains inhabited by Gods, where at last we were led to plants of *Magnolia sieboldii*, growing at the side of a stream alongside such plants as *Stewartia koreana*. The magnolias were not in leaf but the attractions of growing the plant in a

waterside setting were evident. Morale already high, rose further as we continued our journey towards Chollipo, the mecca of magnolias.

Chollipo Arboretum is the creation of Ferris Miller, an American, now naturalized Korean who has lived in Korea for 52 years and who in the 1960s had a vision of an arboretum which he started to implement in 1970. The arboretum now contains a remarkable collection of woody plants and is especially notable for the magnolias and hollies. The magnolia collection alone is one of the most comprehensive in the world with 400 species, hybrids and named cultivars. Chollipo is a fishing and farming village at the tip of the Taean peninsula where the tides are among the highest in the world.

The average annual rainfall is 102cm (40in) although it is unevenly spread through the year with half the annual fall coming between late June and early August. The temperature in winter does not fall below -10°C (14°F) and the first frost comes in mid-November and the last around the middle of March. Spring arrives abruptly with a shift in the prevailing winds from north-west to south-west so there are no late unexpected spring frosts to cause problems.

The result for us was a richness of magnolias in a beautiful coastal setting which few of us had ever experienced elsewhere. It was somewhat invidious to make selections or choices among so many plants that were flowering well. However, if names have to be mentioned *M.* 'Star Wars' (*M. liliiflora* × *M. campbellii*) was a major attraction, particularly when set against a pine background. *M.* 'Iolanthe' (*M. lennei* × *M.* 'Mark Jury') was another that drew our attention.

We subsequently walked through the village to see another part of the collection which included beautiful plants of *Magnolia* 'Galaxy' (*M. liliiflora* 'Nigra' × *M. sprengeri diva*). The dark colour stood out very well and a discussion ensued as to the extent to which a hot sun gave a darker bloom. *M.* 'Elizabeth' with a plaque in memory of Ferris Miller's aunt was one of the finest yellow flowering magnolias that we saw. The plant of the day if not of the tour, was *M.* 'Spectrum' (*M. liliiflora* 'Nigra' × *M. sprengeri diva*) (see Fig. 17); one example was planted most effectively alongside *Prunus serrulata.*

The commitment of the staff at Chollipo to the collection and its curation was deeply impressive under Song Kihun and Chong Mun-Yong. This visit was the centrepiece of our tour and we were all accommodated in great comfort in traditional Korean houses which have been rescued, restored and then sited in different parts of the estate. Our admiration for Ferris Miller who has inspired and brought this collection to its present eminence is unbounded, and we all left Chollipo knowing that we had just seen one of the finest magnolia collections that currently exist anywhere in the world.

ROBIN HERBERT *is a member of the Group and the immediate past president of the RHS*

THE COMPOSITE INDEX

STEPHEN FOX

Nineteen-thirty-nine saw the demise of the Rhododendron Association but, after the war, J B Stevenson lost no time in re-forming a society of rhododendron enthusiasts, this time with the RHS. In November 1946 the first Rhododendron Year Book was published. It contained articles on taxonomy, gardens in the UK and abroad, cultivation and propagation, along with reports on trials, awards and the Annual Show. The succeeding 50 issues have followed the same general format. In 1954, the scope was enlarged to include camellias, and from 1974 magnolias also were included.

The Year Books contain material written by experts and enthusiasts from the UK and elsewhere: remarkably little has lost its interest. As a series, the Year Books make a unique and impressive encyclopedia.

Collecting a complete set requires persistence and luck. It was 20 years before I managed to obtain the two rarest volumes, those for 1950 and 1951-2. As I acquired the Year Books, I built up, on my computer, a combined contents list so that I could browse through the articles by subject or by author. I added 'category' to the listing so that articles of a particular type (such as those on propagation) could be displayed together as a group.

The contents list has its limitations: to find the references to any particular plant, a composite index is needed. To prepare this is a daunting task which for many years I shirked: there are (as I now know) more than 37,000 references to rhododendrons and over 9,000 references to camellias. To copy-type the index pages is unacceptably laborious but, fortunately, there is a less time-consuming alternative. Computers can now 'read' that is, they are capable of optical character recognition, whereby the scanned image of a printed page is analysed into the equivalent sequence of keystrokes. Last year I bought a scanner and set to work. I found few problems with the more recent Year Books but, the older books are poorly printed using typefaces which cause many misreads, for example between '3' and '8', and between 'I, 'l' and '1'. Therefore, I had to proof-read and correct very carefully.

I divided the index into five listings: rhododendrons, camellias, magnolias, other plants, and gardens. Each listing was converted into relational database form, allowing it to be sorted and manipulated as necessary. As the lists grew, it became clear that they contained many anomalies of spelling and nomenclature. For example, *R. wardii* used to be spelt with a capital 'W' which had to be modernized. Other references occur to related plants. These come in three categories: special clones (*wardii*

Ellestee and *wardii Meadow Pond*), obsolete synonyms (or names 'sunk') (*asterocalyx, croceum, gloeoblastum, oresterum, prasinocalyx, wardii × croceum*) and names of disputed validity (*litiense*). For easier reference, I decided to set up groups to contain all three categories, so that a search on any name within a group would yield references to each of the group-members. This required considerable time and research. It was not easy, for example, to find the status of *Rhododendron butyricum*!

The final stage was to package the listings, with suitable search and print-out facilities selectable by menu. The result was a stand-alone database package which, on hard disk, occupies four megabytes but which, when compressed, fits on to a single floppy disk.

The computer version of the Composite Index provides a very quick search on plant names and allows the contents list to be sorted by subject or by author. However, many Group members will prefer to have the Index in traditional printed form. In A4 format, the Composite Index occupies about 190 pages, mostly in double-column.

Copies of the printed version of the Composite Index are obtainable from the Hon Secretary - Mrs Joey Warren, Netherton, Buckland Monachorum, Yelverton, Devon PL20 7NL. The cost is £18 plus £2 for postage and packing. Cheques made out to the Rhododendron, Camellia and Magnolia Group must accompany the order. The arrangements and price for the sale of the diskette version will be announced in the next edition of the Bulletin.

STEPHEN FOX *undertook the creation of the Composite Index at the request of the Executive Committee*

RHODODENDRON AND MAGNOLIA NOTES

Rhododendrons on The Tree Register of the British Isles

In spite of a note inviting members to send in measurements of notable rhododendrons of tree-like proportions to The Tree Register of the British Isles (TROBI) the response to date has been almost non-existent – the one exception being a return from Brodick Castle Gardens on the Isle of Arran.

We feel that this minimal feedback of information might be accelerated if we were to list some interesting examples from the records of TROBI thus setting some kind of target for others to focus upon.

R. grande	Stonefield, Argyll	33ft × 4ft 0in + 3ft 3in	(1992)
R. falconeri	Stonefield, Argyll	30ft × 5ft 2in ++	(1992)
R. arboreum	Stonefield, Argyll	26ft × 7ft 1in	(1992)
R. arboreum cinnamomeum	Stonefield, Argyll	40ft × 4ft 0in	(1992)
R. arboreum	Stonefield, Argyll	42ft × 2ft 6in + 2ft 4in	(1992)
R. arboreum zeylanicum	Arduaine, Argyll	26ft × 2ft 8in + 2ft 2in	(1992)
R. fortunei	Heathersett, Surrey	36ft × 2ft 2in @ 6ft	(1993)
R. 'Polar Bear'	Heathersett, Surrey	33ft × 2ft 0in + 2ft 2in	(1993)
R. 'Cornish Red'	Leonardslee, Sussex	40ft × 3ft 7in	(1993)
R. 'Russelliana Southampronia'	Hants	46ft × 3ft 2in + 2ft 6in	(1993)
R. 'Russelliana Southamptonia'	Hants	42ft × 5ft 9in + 3ft 4in	(1993)
R. arboreum	Castle Kennedy	46ft × 4ft 3in	(1993)
R. arboreum	Castle Kennedy	51ft × 5ft 4in	(1993)
R. arboreum	Castle Kennedy	46ft × 5ft 0in+ 5ft 0in	(1993)
R. arboreum	Castle Kennedy	42ft × 3ft 5in	(1993)
R. kesangiae	Castle Kennedy	10ft × 1ft 6in	(1993)
R. genestierianum	Castle Kennedy	16ft × 1ft 6in + 1ft 7in	(1993)
R. 'Sir Charles Lemon'	Castle Kennedy	46ft × 3ft 4in	(1993)
R. fortunei subsp discolor	Logan House	46ft × 4ft 7in	1993)
R. decorum	Logan House	40ft × 3ft 9in + 3ft 0in	(1993)
R. grande	Logan House	36ft × 3ft 2in	(1993)
R. 'Cornish Red'	Chyverton, Cornwall	46ft × 3ft 1in ++	(1991)
R. ririei	Wakehurst Place, Sussex	26ft × 2ft 0in + 1ft 3in	(1993)
R. barbatum	Lingholm, Cumbria	33ft × –	(1991)
R. arboreum	Balbirnie, Fife	– × 5ft 9in	(1993)
R. arboreum 'Fernhill Silver'	Sandymount, Ireland	42ft × 6ft 2in + 4ft 4in	(1990)
R. argyrophyllum	Belsay Castle	42ft × 4ft 2in	(1986)
R. barbatum	Fairburn, Ross	26ft × 1ft 7in + 1ft 7in	(1987)

R. arboreum	Lwr Combe Royal	42ft × 4ft 7in + 1ft 7in	(1988)
R. 'Polar Bear'	Minterne, Dorset	42ft × 3ft 9in	(1988)
R. 'Loders White'	South Lodge, Sussex	30ft × 3ft 1in	(1985)
R. sino-grande	Trebah, Cornwall	30ft × 4ft 6in	(1984)
R. praestans	Trebah, Cornwall	23ft × 2ft 2in	(1984)
R. arboreum	Singleton Abbey	30ft × 4 ft 3in	(1982)
R. arboreum	Lanhydrock, Cornwall	33ft × 7ft 0in	(1985)
R. arboreum	Brodick, Arran	26ft × 9ft 1in	(1993)
R. macabeanum	Brodick, Arran	30ft × 5ft 8in (@ 3½ft)	(1993)
R. falconeri	Brodick, Arran	30ft × +++	(1993)
R. falconeri	Wakehurst Place, Sussex	23ft × 3ft 8in	(1993)
R. arboreum subsp. *cinnamomeum*	Wakehurst Place, Sussex	30ft × 3ft 1in	(1993)
R. arboreum	Wakehurst Place, Sussex	26ft × 2ft 4in	(1993)
R. arboreum	Wakehurst Place, Sussex	33ft × 2ft 2in + 2ft 1in	(1993)
R. arboreum f. *album*	Wakehurst Place, Sussex	16ft × 1ft 4in	(1993)

If members feel that they have rhododendrons of truly tree-like proportions which may qualify for inclusion on TROBI's records please send in the measurements or, if you feel you need advice, we can possibly send one of our regional volunteer measurers to carry out the task for you. Trees should be measured at breast height (1.5m/5ft from the ground). If trees are multiple-stemmed one should measure the main stems separately indicating the number of stems e.g. a four-stemmed specimen might read as follows: 75cm + 68cm + 120cm + 200cm (2ft 6in + 2ft 3in + 4ft + 6ft).

The largest specimens in girth which TROBI hold on record are all *Rhododendron arboreum*: one at Stonefield, Argyll × 2.2m(7ft 1in), in 1992 another at Brodick Castle, Arran × 2.5m(9ft 1in) in 1993, and finally a tree at Lanhydrock in Cornwall which was × 2.1m(7ft) in 1985. From the above list it appears that the tallest rhododendron in the British Isles is the 15.5m(51ft) tall *Rhododendron arboreum* at Castle Kennedy in Wigtownshire, but if anyone can send in information to prove this to be incorrect we would be very

pleased to have the details. We would particularly recommend members who find themselves in the vicinity of Southampton to stop off at Basset Roundabout on the corner of Little Oak Road, (once the site of Rogers Nurseries) in order to admire the large venerable grove of *R.* 'Russellianum Southamptonia' (*R. arboreum* × *R. catawbiense*) raised by W H Rogers, pre 1932: the best is 14m(46ft) tall (see fig.19).

Any information on big or tall rhododendrons should be sent to TROBI, Mrs P Stevenson, 77a Hall End, Wootton, Beds. MK43 9HP.

TONY AND VICKY SCHILLING,.SCOTLAND

Himalayan Rhododendrons in the Gardens of the Vivian Family

Rhododendrons from the gardens of Clyne Castle are frequently mentioned in present day Rhododendron Show reports, the following notes drawn principally from the *Gardeners Chronicle* describe the cultivation of the genus by the Vivian family from the mid 19th century to the early 20th century.

Rhododendron barbatum first flowered

at Singleton Abbey in 1862 (RW, 1862). Michael Pakenham Edgeworth whose name is commemorated in *R. edgeworthii* and the genus *Edgeworthii*, sent seed of *R. barbatum* to Mrs Vivian of Singleton, Swansea. Why Mrs Vivian should have received seed from Edgeworth is unclear as they appear to have been unrelated. Treseder (1878) noted that *R. barbatum* planted 10 years previously was 4.5m (14ft) tall and had 60 fine trusses of blossom. Other unspecified Himalayan rhododendrons were also in cultivation at a time when Mr James Harris was Head Gardener.

A 'Visitor' (1878) mentions an 8m (25ft) *Magnolia conspicua* and the cultivation of camellias outdoors and in pots. There were two rhododendron gardens with *R. grande* (syn. *R. argenteum*), *R. gibsonii*, *R. falconeri*, *R. dalhousiae*, *R.* 'Countess of Haddington' and *R. edgeworthii*. The second garden near a pinetum was planted with *R. thomsonii*, *R. campanulatum*, *R. barbatum*, Ghent azaleas and hybrid rhododendrons.

Harris (1879) writing in a later article 'Indian Rhododendrons in the open air' mentioned that 20 plants of *R. barbatum* were in the garden in 1879. Specimens of *R. arboreum*, *R. eximium*, *R. falconeri*, *R. grande*, *R. thomsonii*, *R. longifolium* (syn. *R. grande*), *R. hodgsonii*, *R. campanulatum*, *R. dalhousiae*, *R. edgeworthii*, *R. formosum*, *R.* 'Countess of Haddington' and *R.* 'MacNabii' were also cultivated. A note in 1884 mentioned Mrs Vivian's garden at Singleton, where *R. barbatum* 3-4m (10-12ft), *R. falconeri*, *R. eximium* and others were in cultivation (Taffy, 1884). It is interesting to speculate about the source of these plants as no mention of the Vivian name appears in the Kew records of the period when Hooker rhododendrons were being distributed to gardens. Perhaps they were grown from seed supplied by Edgeworth, whose seed collections had also been donated to the Botanic Gardens, Glasnevin, Dublin in 1841.

Pettigrew (1885) stated that the Singleton Garden was famed for its collection of arboreal and hybrid rhododendrons. Rhododendrons were grown in the American garden. Indian azaleas and rhododendrons, in particular, *R.* (syn *Azalea*) 'Fielder's White', *R. edgeworthii*, 'with 100 trusses of white cup shaped flowers in April' and *R.* 'Sesterianum' were cultivated in a greenhouse.

Millais (1917) mentions Singleton near Swansea, a garden owned by Lord Swansea and stated that the *R. barbatum* and *R. eximium* present predated the Hooker introduction of these species.

Clyne Castle, near Swansea, an adjoining Vivian property is described by Millais (1917) and the following rhododendrons were cultivated, *R. dalhousiae*, *R. falconeri*, *R. campanulatum*, *R. barbatum* and *R. grande*. In his second book he mentions *R. dalhousiae* (Millais, 1924). When restoration of the Clyne collection commenced in 1979 *R. arboreum* var. *roseum* and *R. falconeri* were in cultivation (Stokes, 1989).

From these descriptions of the Singleton Gardens, the Vivian family cultivated a comprehensive collection of Himalayan rhododendrons. It would also appear that it was a typical Victorian garden with greenhouses, pinetum and American garden.

References

HARRIS, J (1879). 'Indian Rhododendrons

in the Open Air' *The Gardeners Chronicle,* **XI**: 440.

MILLAIS, J G (1917). *Rhododendrons.* Longmans Green & Co, London.

MILLAIS, J G (1924). *Rhododendrons and the various hybrids.* Longmans Green & Co, London.

PETTIGREW, A (1885). 'Singleton Abbey' *Journal of Horticulture and Cottage Gardener,* **11**: n.s. 200-202.

RW (1862). *'Rhododendron barbatum' The Gardeners Chronicle and Agricultural Gazette,* March 22: 261.

STOKES, I (1989). 'The gardens at Clyne Castle' *Rhododendrons 1988-9 with Magnolias and Camellias,* **41**: 46-48.

TAFFY (1884). 'Mrs Vivians garden at Singleton South Wales', *The Gardeners Chronicle* **XXI**: 345.

TRESEDER, J (1878). '*Rhododendron barbatum',* *Gardeners Chronicle* March 23: 376.

VISITOR, (1978). 'Singleton Abbey' *Journal Horticulture and Cottage Gardener,* **35**: 50-52.

MARY FORREST, DUBLIN

Does *Magnolia* 'Vulcan' have juvenile and adult flowers?

In 1988 David Clulow visited Mark Jury's Nursery in North Taranaki, New Zealand. He acquired scions of magnolias 'Apollo', 'Athene', 'Atlas', and 'Milky Way', but not 'Vulcan' as they had applied for a patent on it, so did not want to release it. David considered seeing *Magnolia* 'Vulcan' as the highlight of his trip, and thought that it was extraordinarily beautiful, and unlike anything he had seen before. As soon as it came on the market the following year he had two plants flown over to England.

My plant was presented to me by Viscount Philip de Spoelberch and Mr van Hoey Smith, in memory of a visit of a group of International Dendrology Society members in 1992. It was a two-year-old grafted plant which grew very fast and fastigiate, and is now 6m (20ft) high. The leaves are dark green, 17cm (6½in) long and 10cm (4in) wide, darker in colour than *M. campbellii mollicomata* 'Lanarth' so leaf colour must be inherited from its other parent *M. liliiflora*.

When it flowered for the first time in 1994 it was a great disappointment. The flowers were small and had six recurved striated outer tepals and six irregularly shaped tepals inside. It made a poor impression on me, and did not really look like a magnolia flower. I could not imagine a magnolia connoisseur like David Clulow being so enthusiastic about such an insignificant flower. I was so disappointed that I put my 'Vulcan' on the list of plants to be discarded.

Last April Mr Graham Rankin came to see my magnolias. I showed him *M.* 'Vulcan' and to my astonishment he discovered in the top of the tree a group of perfectly shaped *campbelli*-type flowers of a brilliant and unique red-purple colour. We now understood why David Clulow raved about it. I have never read about such a phenomenon, but assume that the 'juvenile' flowers will disappear and be replaced by the beautifully shaped adult ones.

Many people may have had the same disappointment that I experienced. My advice is to wait patiently for several years. You will be rewarded with flowers of one of the most beautiful magnolias in existence.

PIET VAN VEEN, SWITZERLAND

The two original plants that were flown over from New Zealand to David Clulow in 1989 were two-year-old grafts. They were sent during our spring and were forced to come into leaf again, unfortunately, one did not survive. The other had one flower the following year (see Fig. 19) and has-flowered every year since. In 1994 it was moved from his garden at Tilgates in Surrey, to the garden at Hascombe Court, Surrey, and is now just under 4m (12ft) in height, and still has diminutive flowers.

In 1993 Duncan & Davies distributed *Magnolia* 'Vulcan' to nurseries around the country, which was the source of the first introductions to British gardens.

GRAHAM RANKIN, SURREY

PHOTOGRAPHIC COMPETITION

There was an extremely good variety of entries for the Competition this year, and this made the Judges' task a far from straightforward one. In the end the unanimous choice as the winner for 1998 was Janet Cubey with her splendid portrait of *R. concatenans* (see fig. 11). She writes 'The photo was taken in 1991 when I was working at Lingholm Gardens in the Lake District. Here it was grown as *R. concatenans* (now normally called *R. cinnabarinum* subsp. *xanthocodon*). Sadly these gardens have been closed to the public for the first time this year (1997)'

Of the runners up Mr C F Taylor pro-duced a delicate portrait of the fine hybrid *R.* 'Betty Wormald' (see fig. 12), taken in his garden in Flintshire. Dr Hargreaves had a striking study of a *R. falconeri* hybrid, possibly *R. falconeri* × *R. macabeanum* (see fig. 13), photographed at Clyne Castle Garden, Swansea, in March 1997. Finally the Judges were much taken by another entry from Mr Taylor – his simple but effective picture of *Magnolia* × *soulangeana* 'Alba Superba' (see fig. 15), taken at Bodnant.

The competition remains popular, so remember to set aside your best slides or prints for entry next year .

The Editor

THE RHODODENDRON TOUR
CORNWALL, 7-12 MAY, 1997

CYNTHIA POSTAN

Once again the Rhododendron Group made its way westwards for a short tour of Cornish gardens. The first of our previous visits was in 1948 after the International Conference at Vincent Square. This year our headquarters were at Budock Vean, near Falmouth, from where we were easily able to visit by coach all the eight gardens selected by Valerie Archibold.

Our first morning was spent at Caerhays where we had the good fortune to be led around the woodlands by Mr Julian Williams and his head gardener, Philip Tregunna. It was here that the first propagation and plantings of Ernest Wilson's and George Forrest's collections were made from seed sent to J C Williams by Veitch early in this century. Where five mature *Nothofagus* blew down in the 1990 gale the space has allowed light to fall on, for instance, *Eucryphia moorei* that had not previously flowered. Alas, the best of the famous magnolias were over, but we saw the huge *M.* × *veitchii*, *M.* 'Elizabeth', one of the good Brooklyn yellows and *Michelia doltsopa*, lemon-scented and white-flowered. Others were *Magnolia* 'Star Wars' (first flowered here in 1995), *M. dealbata*, *M. nitida* with coppery young foliage and *M. salicifolia*. Among the rare and tender rhododendron species were *R.*

stenaulum (Section Choniastrum, see *Rhododendrons 1991*, p. 40) and *R. stamineum*, alas neither in flower. Also a flowering *R. minus* var. *chapmanii* (Sect. Carolinianum) about 2 × 2.5m (6 × 8ft). We noted the splendid Caerhays hybrid 'Michael's Pride' (*R. burmanicum* × *R. dalhousiae* var. *dalhousiae*), now rarely seen, but, according to Peter Cox, available in New Zealand. Another striking dwarf in flower was the *R. yakushimanum* hybrid, 'Hydon's Dawn'. One of the glories of Caerhays is the mature woodland setting in which are so many unusual trees such as *Quercus oxyodon*, *Q. lamellosa* and a New Zealand *Hoheria*, to flower later in the summer. There were still many camellias out in this home of *Camellia williamsii*, the mould-breaking parent of so many vigorous hybrids, and especially the excellent Tregrehan hybrids, bred in Cornwall by Miss Carlyon.

Our next visit was to a totally new and different garden. Lamorran House in St Mawes, standing at the head of a cliff overlooking the estuary of the Fal, has been created in the last 20 years by Mr Dudley Cooke, a member of the Group who used to live in Sussex. The garden, originally only 0.4ha (1 acre) around the house, is now much larger and has been extended down almost to the water's edge. Closely planted with trees and shrubs to resemble a Mediterranean garden, you descend the steep hillside by a series of curving steps and paths. Strong architectural features give a coherent structure to what might otherwise become, in the soft Cornish climate, a jungle of vegetation. Everywhere are southern and exotic plants, many of them evergreen, almost all, one might think marginally hardy, but striking in form. Rhododendrons are there, but do not dominate. Palm-like silhouettes such as tree ferns (*Dicksonias*) and Chusan palms are the main icons. We were guided by Mark Brent, the head gardener, and we left a token of our gratitude in the shape of the beautiful yellow-flowered *R.* 'Hotei'.

On Friday, 9 May, we were within walking distance of two famous gardens, Trebah and Glendurgan, both of them dating back to the 1840s and both created by the extraordinary Fox family. At Trebah three generations followed Charles Fox through his daughter Sarah to her son Sir Jonathan Backhouse. The Hext family bought it in 1906, whose last worthy member, Alice, died in 1939. The garden leading down to the private beach on the Helford River had its moment of glory during the preparations for D Day, but it was not until Mr and Mrs Hibbert bought the property in 1981 that its place in the history of gardening in Cornwall was recovered. Now the subject of a charitable trust, as all great gardens should be, its old original features are preserved, while new plantings and ideas are happily blended in. The site, which bears more than a resemblance to a Himalayan rain forest, is a narrow heavily planted glen falling steeply from the terrace by the house. It is watered by a stream dammed up from time to time into pools for aquatic plants. The tender, scented species and hybrid rhododendrons form the main collection at this time of the year, together with huge specimens of unusual conifers and magnolias lining the steep protective banks of the glen. In flower for us was an eyecatching combination of an indigo blue *Ceanothus* 'Concha' and a lime green *Euphorbia*. We were all grateful to Tony Hibbert for welcoming us and hoped he would like the rare *Daphne bholua* Valerie had found. Could this be one plant he does not already have?

Our afternoon visit to nearby Glendurgan, another Fox garden, made an interesting contrast: the same situation but so different. The feeling is more spacious and open, there are grassy glades to encourage wild flowers, and the tree cover (although still primarily a protection from wind) is less dominant. The old tender Cornish rhododendron hybrids abound, such as 'Budock', 'Barclayi', 'Beauty of Tremough', etc, but in the 30s Cuthbert Fox planted extensively Asiatic rhododendrons, magnolias, cornus, camellias and eucryphias. Remarkable specimens included the huge *Drimys winteri* and the fantastic elephantine trunk of the *Liriodendron tulipifera*.

On Saturday the coach took us to Tregothnan, another of the historic gardens of the county, where Lady Falmouth was waiting to welcome us. The fascination of garden-visiting is the contrast of settings. Tregothnan, a magnificent mock-Tudor mansion, lies on high ground with views of the Falmouth estuary. It is isolated on its own peninsula and is surrounded by a seemingly limitless space in which the generations have created a horticultural paradise. The old garden has been described before (*Rhododendron Year Book*, 1949, p. 124, *ibid*, 1968, p. 1). Humphrey Repton in 1809 began the alterations with shelter belts to the south-west and a walk of *Camellia japonica*. The Boscawen family, allied to that of the 17th-century sylviculturist John Evelyn, has in the last century extended and developed the garden area to make it perhaps one of the largest and most comprehensive in the county. Among the mid-19th century plantings are believed to be a huge unnamed white camellia and there have been many more of the genus in the present century including, after 1956, modern cultivars of *C. japonica* and *C. williamsii*. Around the house are terraces with formal beds, all of which contain enviably tender plants and shrubs. However, as Lady Falmouth emphasises, frost is by no means unknown and wind the ever-present enemy.

For many of us the so-called 'new' arboretum was of absorbing interest. Here, in a large area where recent notorious gales had wreaked great damage, there has been the opportunity to plant many young trees, including conifers such as the tender *Pinus patulum*. Of immense age, was the massive cork oak (*Quercus suber*), its corky bark rivalling a piece of modern sculpture. Rhododendrons, many of them dating back over a hundred years, must not be omitted: members of the group noted *R. arboreum* subsp. *delavayi* and *R. trichostomum* among many, many others in flower. Also *Azara microphylla* and *Cornus florida rubra*. We were joined at this point by Lord Falmouth and after our long walk we were refreshed with sherry and had time to talk to our kind

host and hostess. To add to their collection of magnolias, we were delighted to present one – *M.* 'Yellow Bird' – which may be a newcomer.

Then, a short drive to Trewithen at Grampound. This is perhaps the best-known of the Cornish private gardens as it is open to the public six days of the week. It is justly famous and the Rhododendron Group owes much to its creator, George Johnstone, who was one of the original members of the 1915 Rhododendron Society (and author of *Asiatic Magnolias in Cultivation* published by the RHS in 1955). Needless to say, Trewithen garden contains examples of all the most sought after magnolia species and named cultivars. The selective list of Trewithen plants names 23 magnolias, including four different *M. campbellii*. There is *M. sargentiana* var. *robusta*, so called by Dr Alfred Rehder. In 1908 'Chinese' Wilson brought back seed to the Arnold Arboretum. In 1913 it was propagated by grafts in France and distributed in 1919 to a number of the milder British gardens (Walter Magor in *Rhododendrons*, 1988/89, p. 62).

There are of course many other famous plants in the garden, many of which are displayed in the curved plantings beside the great lawn considered a masterpiece of landscape design. There are the Trewithen hybrids, 'Alison Johnstone', Trewithen Orange' and 'Blue Riband', many of the Triflorum section, such as *R. davidsonianum* and *R. yunnanense*, a fine *R.* 'Hotei' to compare with its rival *R.* 'Crest' and, too late for its famous yellow flowers, a sadly reduced *R. macabeanum*, the pride of the garden (see G Johnstone, *The Rhododendron Year Book*, 1950, p. 99).

On Sunday, 11 May we drove to Cornwall's north-west, below Bodmin Moor and slightly less favoured in climate. Our morning visit was to Tremeer, another private garden with many resonances for our Group. This garden, relatively youthful by Cornish standards, was the creation of General Eric Harrison who settled here on his retirement after the last war, soon becoming deeply involved with the cultivation of rhododendrons. In 1961 he married Mrs Roza Stevenson, widow of John Barr Stevenson, owner of Tower Court, Ascot, and editor of *The Species of Rhododendron*, published by the Rhododendron Society in 1930. She took many cuttings and plants from Tower Court with her to Tremeer, including some Kurume azaleas, obtained from Wada in Japan and said to be better than the 'Wilson Fifty'. Roza died in 1967 but General Harrison remained at Tremeer until 1977. The house and garden are now owned by the Haslam-Hopwood family. The garden is best known for the cultivars of the 'Blue Tit' grex (*R. augustinii* × *R. impeditum*) bred by J C Williams at Caerhays. General Harrison grew cuttings from nearby Lamellen and obtained FCCs for the clones 'Saint Breward' and 'Saint Tudy'; backcrossed with their parents they produced 'Saint Kew' (PC in 1970) and 'Saint Merryn' (FCC in 1986). All these now produce a great show at Tremeer. Their remarkable record of awards is 4 FCCs, 9 AMs and 3 PCs. We saw in flower 'Actress', ('Lady Alice Fitzwilliam' × *R. edgeworthii*), heavily scented, white splashed with crimson outside, another Harrison hybrid, and 'Day Dream', cream with flesh-coloured eye.

Our last visit was to Pencarrow, where we were welcomed by Sir Arscott and Lady Molesworth St Aubyn and given a delicious lunch in the stables. As well as wine on the tables there were trusses of rhododendrons which we were challenged to identify. The garden is another historic one dating back to the 1840s and created by Sir William Molesworth, a rich radical politician. He built the Italian garden with rocks moved from the moors above by his tenants who were rewarded with a six-months rent holiday. The formal garden, best seen from the slopes of the park, is but one feature in the 20.25ha (50 acres): there are also the Victorian garden and the rock garden through which the way leads up by the stream and woodland glen – another Himalayan looka-like. Some of the greatest treasures are here, including most of the 650 different rhododendrons. Species noted in flower were *R. trichostomum* and *R. fortunei*. Hybrids noted were 'Idealist', 'September Song', 'Gwillt King', 'Yvonne Pride' and the old Mangles 'Beauty of Littleworth'. All very striking. Impossible also not to mention the collection of unusual conifers, such as *Athrotaxis* × *laxifolia*, a Tasmanian cedar, now considered a hybrid and the huge golden beech (*Fagus sylvatica* 'Zlatia') standing supreme in the park. Alter a splendid cream tea we presented 'Mole' and Iona with a *Cupressus torulosa cashmeriana* which we hoped would grow to be worthy of its site and companions. Thus ended the 1997 tour, made possible by Valerie's unobtrusive organisation.

CYNTHIA POSTAN *was Hon. Editor of the Year Book from 1988 until 1997, and also edited* The Rhododendron Story *in 1996*

The world of rhododendron competition, at least at Vincent Square, was turned upside-down this year.

The early competition, for so long a dismal Cinderella to the main show, was favoured by a fairy godmother of a spring while the latter event was all but massacred by an ugly frost which struck about a week before the April show took place. The result was that the early competition sensationally became the bigger affair, with significantly more exhibits and an extraordinary display of flower, that one would not normally expect to see in mid-March. Unusually precocious were *R. campylocarpum*, *R. hodgsonii*, *R. adenogynum* and perhaps *R. glischroides*. Unusually interesting was to see such blooms in the company of the early flowering types such as *R. dauricum*, and 'Christmas Cheer'.

But whatever joy we took from the early competition was somewhat dashed by what was to befall the main competition: entries were so few that it took only two show benches to accommodate them and close to half the 58 classes went uncontested. Having said this, however, it must be reported that those who did take part made a fist of it and, in spite of the frost, produced several surprisingly good vases and a collection of blooms that usually open long after this particular contest is over.

The Cups

The Loder Challenge Cup for the best hybrid was won this year by Mr Richard Gilbert from Bodmin in Cornwall. There are three other cups awarded at the main Rhododendron Competition and these are: The McLaren Challenge Cup for the best

The Loder Cup

species truss. The Roza Stevenson Challenge cup for the best species spray and the Crosfield Challenge Cup for three hybrids bred and raised in the garden of the exhibitor.

In the Main Camellia Show, The Leonardslee Bowl is awarded as first prize in the 12 bloom class.

These impressive trophies have been competed for since the 1920s and 30s and over the years have been won by some of the country's most notable gardens and gardeners.

BRIAN WRIGHT, SUSSEX

The Early Rhododendron Show
18-19 March, 1997

After several very lean years The Early Rhododendron Competition was well supported by exhibitors who made more than three times as many entries as were shown in 1996 and five times as many as in 1995. After a colder than average spell in January the weather was mild in many parts of the country for several weeks before the Show and this undoubtedly allowed for more plants to be in bloom with a correspondingly greater choice of entries for the exhibitors, chief of whom must be mentioned – Nymans Garden (The National Trust) in Sussex – who contributed a third of all the entries and dominated the species classes (Nos. 1 to 11). Not surprisingly therefore the standard of many entries was high and of some it was superb, with Class 2 perhaps the most spectacular of all.

Class 1, for three species – one truss of each, was won by The City of Swansea (Clyne Gardens) with a well-balanced group of *R. sutchuenense*, *R. beanianum* and *R. uvarifolium*. Nymans Garden gained second prize with an equally well-balanced group of *R. fulvum*, *R. principis* and *R. adenogynum*,

all of which showing their attractive foliage as a bonus. Nymans also gained the third prize.

Class 2, for a spray of a species, attracted seven entries with first prize going to Nymans for their *R. glischroides* with no less than 17 perfect trusses (all within the size limitation imposed by the schedule). If there had been a prize for 'best in show' this must surely have won it. Swansea gained second prize with a lovely spray of a pink *R. arboreum* with 8 perfect trusses while Nigel Holman had to be content with third prize for his *R. macabeanum* which had only 6 perfect trusses. A splendid class.

Class 3, for one truss of a species, attracted eight entries with four prizes deservedly being awarded; the first to Nymans for *R. macabeanum* KW 7724, second also to Nymans for *R. pocophorum*; third prize to Swansea's *R. hodgsonii* (see fig. 20) and Nymans the fourth with *R. uvarifolium*.

Class 4, for a species in Subsects. Arborea or Argyrophylla, one truss, was won by Nymans with *R. arboreum*, which species also gained second prize for Swansea, while the third went to Nymans for *R. floribundum*.

Class 5, for a truss of a species in the Subsects. Barbata, Glischra or Maculifera was again won by Nymans, but second and third went to Swansea.

Class 6, for a truss from Subsects. Falconera or Grandia showed *R. macabeanum* gaining the first two prizes for Nymans and Nigel Holman respectively, with a splendid truss of *R. hodgsonii* TSS 9 only awarded the third prize for its collector, Maj. Tom Spring-Smyth.

Class 7, for a truss of Subsect. Fortunea was won by Heaselands Garden (Sir Richard Kleinwort) with a delightful *R. sutchuenense*, which species also gained second prize for Swansea with Nymans third for their *R. oreodoxa*.

Class 8, for a spray of Subsect. Neriiflora had eight entries with the honours shared equally between Swansea with first and fourth prizes, while Nymans gained second and third in a plethora of good reds.

Class 9, for a spray from several subsections which used to be lumped under the Thomsonii Series (Balfour), had only three entries all from Nymans who were awarded the three prizes.

Class 10, for a spray from a host of 16 subsections had nine entries with Dr R Jack winning first prize for his *R. dauricum* 'White Hokkaido' (Subsect. Rhodorastra), second prize to Nymans with *R. sulphureum* (Subsect. Boothia) and third prize also to Nymans for a spray of *R. racemosum* of very dubious pedigree both for flower colour and foliage which showed none of the characteristic white on the underside of the leaves.

Class 11, for any other species not covered in the foregoing classes (one truss), had eight of the nine entries all from Nymans who won all four prizes.

Classes 12 and 13 had no entries.

Class 14, for a spray of any hybrid, had five entries but only two prizes were awarded, the first going to Nymans for a superb 'Seta', a great favourite in the early spring garden, while another long-established favourite 'Christmas Cheer' won second prize for Swansea.

Class 15, for a truss of any hybrid. was won by Swansea with a fine but un-named

R. macabeanum hybrid, with second going to Nymans and third to Dr J Dayton.

Class 16, for a truss of a hybrid of which one parent must be from a list of a host of nine subsections species was won by Swansea with 'Cornubia' with second prize to Dr R Jack.

Class 17 had no entries.

Class 18, for a truss of any elepidote hybrid, of which neither parent may be from a list of 10 subsections species, was supported only by Swansea who gained the two prizes for their Grandia hybrids in which *R. macabeanum* predominated.

Classes 19 and 20 were a complete muddle because the showbench labels were numbered the opposite way round from the show schedule of classes. An attempt by the stewards to correct the error had only made matters worse, with the result that clepidote and lepidote hybrids were mixed up in each others class; there was the absurd spectacle of the hybrid 'Yellow Hammer' being awarded a prize in the elepidote section, for example. Other entries included a fine *R. flavidum* and a good *R.* 'Emasculum' and 'Pematit' with the most unusual and certainly seldom seen 'Rose Vallon' shown by Dr R Jack, with its maroon-purple underside to the leaves, attracting much interest.

Class 21, for a truss of a tender species or hybrid was won by Dr Jack with *R. ciliicalyx*. Dr J Dayton won the other prizes from his four entries.

Class 22, for a spray of a tender plant grown under glass or otherwise had two entries – both species – with first prize going to Dr Jack with *R. hongkongense* and second to Brian Wright for his *R. burmanicum*.

DAVID FARNES, DERBYSHIRE

The Main Rhododendron Show: Species 29-30 April 1997

In my report of the species classes at the 1996 show, I was full of optimism, as it was the best show for a number of years, and I questioned we might see a renewal of interest in the genus.

We must continue to hope, however, as this year's show was a victim of cruel, late frost, especially damaging to magnolias, camellias and rhododendrons and this caused many of our regular exhibitors to withdraw. Entries were down in all classes, nevertheless there were some sprays and trusses of good quality.

Class 1, six species, one truss of each – no entry.

Class 2, three species, one truss of each – one entry from High Beeches Conservation Trust consisting of *R. vernicosum*, *R. arboreum* and *R. fictolacteum* – worthy of the first prize awarded.

Class 3, any species, one truss – here the McLaren Challenge Cup was won by Brian Wright of Crowborough with a very clean and well-presented *R. aberconwayi*, followed by High Beeches with *R. vernicosum* and, in third place was *R. yakushimanum* 'Angel' from the same garden.

Class 4, any species, one spray. The winner receiving the Roza Stevenson Challenge Cup was High Beeches with a very good spray of *R. oreotrephes*. *R. arboreum album* from the same exhibitor was placed second, with the Isabella Plantation, Richmond Park, a close third with a very pleasing vase of *R. anhweiense*.

Class 5, any species of Subsect. Arborea or Subsect. Argyrophylla – only one entry from Brian Wright of *R. arboreum*, a single truss.

Classes 6 and 7, no entries.

Class 8, any species of Subsect. Grandia or Subsect. Falconeri, one truss. A very well-shaped and clean *R. fictolacteum* from High Beeches was the only entry.

Class 9, any species of Subsect. Fortunea, one truss – the only entry being *R. orbiculare* from Brian Wright.

Class 10, any species of Subsect. Fulva, Subsect. Irrorata or Subsect. Parishia, one truss. A truss of *R. aberconwayi* equally as good as the one in Class 3 was a winner for the same exhibitor Brian Wright.

Class 11, any species of Subsect. Taliensia, one truss – again only one entry, a very clean *R. roxieanum* var. *oreonastes* from High Beeches.

The following six classes failed to draw any entries.

Class 18, any species of Subsect. Edgworthia or Subsect. Maddenia, one spray. The only entry was from Dr Dayton of Dorking exhibiting a small, but undamaged *R. edgworthii*.

Class 19, any species of Subsect. Maddenia ('Dalhousiae-Alliance' and 'Megacalyx-Alliance' only), one truss. A near-perfect truss worthy of the first it received was *R. lindleyi*, well shown by Dr Jack from Scotland.

Class 20, any species of Subsect. Triflora and Subsect. Heliolepida other than *R. augustinii*, one spray. First place was awarded to High Beeches with *R. ambiguum*, only just beating a very pretty spray of the same species, labelled *R. chengshienianum*.

Class 21, no entries.

Class 22, any species of Subsect. Cinnabarina, Subsect. Tephropepla or Subsect. Virgata, one spray – High Beeches provided the only two entries. First prize went to a lovely spray of *R. xanthocodon*, only just beating *R. concatenans*.

Class 23, any species of Subsect. Campylogyna, Subsect. Genistieriana, or Subsect. Glauca, one spray – the only entry was from High Beeches showing *R. glaucophyllum*.

Class 24, any species of Subsect. Lapponica, one spray – second was Dr Jack with *R. fastigiatum*, only just behind the *R. polycladum* from High Beeches.

No entries in Classes 25-29.

Class 30, any species of deciduous Azalea, one spray. A clear pink spray of *R. vaseyi* gained the first prize card, the second went to *R. roseum* – both exhibits being from High Beeches.

Class 31, any species of evergreen Azalea, one spray. Perhaps the most colourful vase in the show was the *R. kaempferi* in this class from High Beeches. This is evergreen in the south, but not further north. What a pity it was the only entry.

I must mention the two fine trade stands of rhododendrons at the show. What a pleasure to see the Gold Medal exhibit from Knaphill and Slococks Nurseries on a large stand, with such old favourites as *R.* 'Susan', *R.* 'Countess of Athlone', *R.* 'Lady Grey Egerton', large trusses of *R.* 'Lavender Girl', and taking the centre stage, the interesting *R.* 'Pink Rosette' – with its ring of petaloids in the centre of each flower.

Matthewmans of Pontefract enhanced the show with a display of compact growing rhododendrons suitable for the smaller garden – *R.* 'Arctic Tern', *R.* 'Egret', *R.* 'Chikor' and *R.* 'Ruby Heart' – a floriferous,

scarlet improvement on *R.* 'Carmen'. May we hope to see these interesting stands again next year.

ARCHIE SKINNER, SUSSEX

The Main Rhododendron Show: Hybrids

As well as thinning the whole of the hybrid section, the frost also left 10 of the 27 classes without any entries whatsoever. This report, therefore, mentions only those classes that contained competitive exhibits.

Class 32 for six hybrid trusses attracted one entry - a feisty collection comprising 'Susan', 'The Earl of Athlone', 'Roza Stevenson', 'Marie Curie', 'Loder's White' and 'Loderi King George'. This group, fresh and virtually unblemished, deservedly won a first prize for the West Sussex garden of High Beeches.

Class 33 for three hybrid trusses gave us three entries with the first prize going to Richard Gilbert of Bodmin who offered a trio of good yellows in 'Hotei', 'Roza Stevenson' and 'Buckland Beauty'. Second was Isabella Plantation, Richmond Park, London, with 'Naomi Hope' and two well advanced old ironclads in 'Cynthia' and 'Old Port'. High Beeches were third with their home-raised 'Hullaballoo', 'Armistice Day' and 'Manglesii', an old Veitch hybrid which gained an FCC in 1885.

Class 34 for any hybrid truss is the most popular class in the show. Usually it attracts between 20 and 30 entries and awards the Loder Challenge Cup to the best of these. This year the exhibits were down to nine with the Cup going to Cornwall in the hands of Bodmin's Richard Gilbert who exhibited a worthy 'Roza Stevenson'. Runner-up was Brian Wright of Crowborough, East Sussex, who showed the American hybrid 'Halfdan Lem', a plant whose scarlet trusses usually open much too late for this show. In third place came High Beeches with another good 'Roza Stevenson'.

Class 35 for any hybrid spray. Although this class displayed four entries only two were awarded prizes. Both went to Dr John Dayton from Dorking, Surrey who achieved a first with a fine 'Hawk Crest' and a second with an unnamed exhibit with attractive lanceolate foliage.

Class 37 for Loderi group trusses showed three exhibits. None was felt good enough to be awarded first prize but second prize went to Brian Wright for 'Loderi King George' and third to Richard Gilbert for 'Loderi Pink Diamond'.

Class 38 for one truss of any hybrid parently related to Subsect. Fortunea was won by Brian Wright who showed 'Susan'. High Beeches who also showed 'Susan' were second and Brian Wright third with 'Luscombei Splendens'.

Class 39 for one spray parently linked to *williamsianum* was won by Brian Wright who entered 'Moerheim's Pink', a Dietrich Hobbie creation. This was the only entry.

Class 40 for trusses with one parent being of Subsect. Campylocarpa produced three entries. First was Brian Wright's 'Carita Inchmery' followed by two vases of 'Carita Golden Dream' - one from Dr. John Dayton which was awarded second prize and the other from Brian Wright, given third.

Class 41. Brian Wright produced the sole entry for trusses of Neriiflora blood. It was 'Scarlet Wonder' which was awarded first prize.

Class 42 for *thomsonii* offspring saw

Brian Wright scoop first and second prizes with 'Hawk Crest' and 'Pride of Leonardslee'. High Beeches' 'Hullaballoo' took third.

Class 46 for trusses of which one parent is of Subsect. Pontica was won by Brian Wright showing 'Cunningham's White'. This was placed ahead of a colourful ponticum seedling exhibited by Dr Dayton.

Class 49 for the tender maddenia and edgeworthia progeny attracted four entries. It was well won by Dr Robbie Jack from Lanark who presented the attractive 'Fragrantissimum' which goes back to 1868. Runner-up was Mr Alan Hardy from Hythe in Kent who showed 'Jane Hardy', his own exotic *nuttallii* and *lindleyii* cross.

Class 50 for sprays of which one parent is of Subsect. Triflora gave us only one entry, an unnamed *augustinii* hybrid which was awarded a second prize for High Beeches.

Class 51 for trusses of Lepidote hybrids not covered by previous classes also attracted only one entry. As a Vireya, however, it was well worth seeing and well worth the first prize it won for Mr Alan Hardy.

Class 56 was another class that could muster only a single entry. It called for hybrid sprays grown under glass and produced a fine specimen of 'Fragrantissimum' which gained a first prize for Dr Dayton.

Class 57 for evergreen azaleas rewarded the Isabella Plantation with a hat-trick of prizes for an attractive display of 'Irohayama', 'Palestrina' and 'Blaauw's Pink'.

Class 58 for deciduous azaleas was won by Isabella Plantation showing a nice yellow/orange Ghent called 'Unique'. The only other entry was given NAS for being rather more evergreen than deciduous.

BRIAN WRIGHT, SUSSEX

THE CAMELLIA SHOWS

CICELY PERRING

The spring of 1997 was a cruel one for the camellia. The cultivars showed their objection by withholding their flowers until much later than usual; then when they finally succumbed they suffered warm, bright days followed by bitterly cold and frosty nights which blackened flowers, buds and leaves. Of course, not only camellias suffered. Rhododendrons and magnolias were equally affected. As a result the exhibits at the shows of this year have been reduced, and the damage sustained caused real grief.

The Early Show 18th March, 1997
Sprays
Class 1, there were seven entries and of these Mr K T Powell of London produced for a first a wonderful spray of 'Ruddigore' grown in the open. The flowers were in pristine condition and it was a really beautiful entry. Second came 'Margaret Davis' grown indoors, such a beautiful camellia, shown by Mrs V H P Bettley from Kent, and third – again from the open – 'Italiana' shown by Marigold Assinder from London. Chiswick House produced from indoors a very lovely camellia, red with melding blotches of pink/white. While the name is unknown, it richly deserved being highly commended. This class was most satisfactory, although six entries down on 1996.

Class 2, only two entries. A first went to Marigold Assinder with a really lovely spray of 'Brigadoon' from the open, with a second to D R Strauss for 'Debbie', grown indoors.

Class 3, two entries. 'Ming Temple' with wonderfully crumpled petals was first shown by Mrs Bettley and grown indoors, and second was 'Dorothy James' by D R Strauss, again indoors but hardly open.

Overall the sprays were not inspiring, with the exception of 'Ruddigore'.

Single Blooms
After the sprays the remaining classes are devoted to single blooms. The Duke of Devonshire, Mr D R Strauss, Marigold Assinder, Mr and Mrs Short, J Newman, Chiswick House, Mr and Mrs Bettley, A W Simons and Mr D Davies were all successful.

Mr D R Strauss exhibited *Camellia chrysantha*, a lovely yellow bloom so different from the camellias we know.

Mostly the winning blooms were from cultivars well known and old favourites. Only one example of 'Donation', 'Carnation' and 'Augusto l'Gouveia Pinto', all much more prominent in previous years. 'Wildfire' has increased in popularity, and the Duke of Devonshire exhibited 'Gwynneth Morey', very similar to 'Brushfields Yellow' but more attractive.

Class 13 was exceptional, with 17 entries showing a wonderful range of blooms from 'Drama Girl', large and bountiful, to 'Fleur Dipater', small and dainty.

Interesting too was the range of blooms grown outside as against those grown under glass, the latter more plentiful but the former were quite as fine.

In spite of the difficulties it was a good show. How indebted we are to all those who entered their blooms, whether or not they won a placement. Without them there would be no competition or show, and the delight of those viewing the blooms on the bench was very rewarding. As always we have to thank the never-failing help and kindness of the RHS staff, who contribute so much to the success of this show.

The Main Camellia Show, 15th April 1997

The weather had not been any kinder, and it was remarkable that such a splendid display could be mounted – a great credit to the exhibitors.

The great attraction of this show is the competition for the Leonardslee Bowl. The entry is any 12, one bloom of each, and it came under Class 10. There were nine entries involving 108 perfect blooms, even if some were more perfect than others. 'Nuccio's Jewel' figured in three of the winning exhibits and 'Captain Rawes' in two. Otherwise there was a wide range. of cultivars. The winner was Ann Hooten (see fig. 21). Mrs C Petherick came second, A W Simons third, Exbury Gardens fourth; Highly Commended, Stonehurst Gardens, and Commended, Marigold Assinder. Included in her entry was a very lovely specimen of 'Grand Jury'. For special mention also: 'Miss Charleston' in the prize-winning

entry and the positioning of 'Joan Trehane' next to 'Te Deum' in the second placement.

The five classes in division 1 for sprays only attracted 11 entries overall. Particularly good was the entry of Ann Hooten in Class 1 with three lovely sprays: 'Rose Parade', 'Bridal Gown' and especially 'Miss Charleston', with five exquisite blooms. Ann Hooten did particularly well in this class, gaining four firsts and one second. Congratulations.

The next most testing class is number 11, which requires six blooms. There were eight entries. David Davis came first with a fine show of 'Nuccio's Jewel', 'Tiffany' (a lovely fresh flower with beautiful leaves), 'Elegans', 'Shiro Chan', 'Giulio Nuccio' and 'Kramer's Supreme'. Second was Ann Hooten, third Mrs C Petherick and fourth Exbury Gardens. 'Nuccio's Jewel' figured twice and 'Tiffany' twice, otherwise all different cultivars.

In Class 12 for single-flowered cultivars Mrs Petherick came first, and in her entry was a delightful newcomer to the show: 'Shino Akebono', a shell-pink 'Hego' type of fragile beauty. Ann Hooten came first in Class 13 and Mr and Mrs Short second with a fine example of 'Adelina Patti'.

Class 14, this class was for any three semi-double cultivars, one bloom of each, and first was Ann Hooten. However, there was one bloom in the entry of Mrs C Petherick, who was unplaced, that was most lovely and not generally exhibited: 'Edelweiss' – quite memorable and interesting. She came second in Class 15 with another bloom of 'Edelweiss'. Mr and Mrs Short were placed first with 'Bob Hope', a wonderful red which should be in every collection. There were 20 superb entries in this class.

Class 16 was notable in that 'Nuccio's Jewel' was exhibited in the first, second and third placements. The class required three anemone-formed or peony-formed cultivars.

David Davis came first, Ann Hooten second, Exbury Gardens third and A W Simons fourth. In the entry of Mrs Petherick was a bloom of 'Warrior', a wonderful dark red which is becoming popular.

Class 17 attracted 15 entries. First was 'Elizabeth Dowd' shown by Ann Hooten, another lovely new camellia to our show bench, although not a new cultivar. 'Nuccio's Jewel' exhibited by David Davis came second and again exhibited by Ann Hooten third. Surely 'Nuccio's Jewel' must have been the most popular camellia of the 1997 shows.

Class 18 for rose-formed and formal double cultivars of *C. japonica* brought out all the favourites, and Ann Hooten, Exbury Gardens and A W Simons were placed in that order.

Class 19, which attracted 17 entries, was as Class 18 but one bloom, not three. First were Mr and Mrs Short with 'Tomorrow Park Hill', also second with 'In the Pink'. Third was Barbara Waterlow and fourth Doreen M Wernick with 'Joseph Pfingstl'. Highly Commended was Mrs Petherick with 'Glen 40', another lovely red.

Class 20. First and second came Ann Hooten's entries: 'Elegant Beauty', 'Wilbur Foss', 'Dr Clifford Parks', 'Satan's Robe', 'Nora Jury' and 'Anticipation' – a superb feat to produce six such lovely blooms. Third, Mrs C Petherick entered 'Elegant Beauty', 'Anticipation' and 'Royalty', and fourth, J Newman with 'Mary Phoebe Taylor',

'Brushfields Yellow' and 'Milshoka'.

Class 21. Ann Hooten exhibiting 'Dr Clifford Parks' came first, Marigold Assinder's 'Captain Rawes' second and A W Simons' 'Valentine's Day' third.

Classes 22, 23, 24, 25 and 26 were the turn of the *williamsii* cultivars, the most generally grown and good-tempered of the camellia world. David Davis, Ann Hooten, Exbury Gardens, Mr and Mrs Short and A W Simons were all placed, and favourites such as 'Debbie', 'Elegant Beauty', 'Waterlily', 'Anticipation', 'Julia Hamiter', 'Elsie Jury' and 'Donation' figured among the entries.

Class 27. There were five most interesting entries, which was for any species or hybrid not otherwise specified. The class was won by P J Mackworth-Praed with an unnamed seedling. The bloom was like a small Lady Vansittart. Second was J Newman also with an unnamed seedling, and third P J Mackworth-Praed with another seedling, all encouraging for future exhibits.

We missed John Tooby with the delightful seedling from 'Garnet Gleam', which showed such promise.

Although reduced by the inclement weather, it was a very fine show and great credit to those exhibitors who go to such trouble to prepare and display their blooms. It is very good that, slowly, new cultivars are being shown, although it is mostly the old favourites from well-established bushes which take first place. Every season brings a new challenge to the growers, and we need to extend the challenge to more of the camellia enthusiasts and persuade them to exhibit their blooms.

CICELY PERRING, SUSSEX.

AWARDS 1997

Award of Merit

Rhododendron **'Leo'** (evergreen azalea) ('Malvaticum' × *R. kaempferi*). AM, 19 May 1997, as a hardy flowering plant for exhibition. Trusses of 1-6 flowers. Corolla funnel-shaped to 40mm long and 50mm wide, 5-lobed. Corolla uniformly red (43B) with slightly darker spotting on inside of upper lobes. Stamens 5, slightly protruding; filaments red, pubescent at base; anthers black. Stigma brown; style red with long hairs at base; ovary villous. Calyx green, with 5 distinct hairy lobes each 6 × 3mm. Pedicel to 1cm, densely hairy. Leaves adjacent to inflorescence oblanceolate to obovate, 20 × 10mm, pubescent above and more densely so beneath. New leaves larger. Raised by Mr L de Rothschild. Exhibited by Mr E de Rothschild, Exbury Gardens, Exbury, Hampshire SO45 1AZ. Specimen and transparency in Herb. Hort. Wisley.

Rhododendron **'Naomi Astarte'** ('Aurora' × *R. fortunei* subsp. *fortunei*). AM, 19 May 1997, as a hardy flowering plant for exhibition. Trusses of *c.* 7 flowers, loose, to 180mm across. Corolla funnel-campanulate, to 70mm long and 70mm wide, 7 slightly retuse lobes. Corolla pinkish purple (64C) in bud; throat and mouth pale yellow (8C-D), deepening to pink (65C) on lobes and outside. Stamens 14-15, held within; filaments white; anthers brown. Style and stigma green; style glandular at base; ovary glandular. Calyx rudimentary, 2-5mm, green.

Leaves oblong to oblanceolate, 120 × 50mm, hairless, matt green above, pale green below; petioles reddish brown. Raised by Mr E de Rothschild. Exhibited by Mr E de Rothschild, Exbury Gardens, Exbury, Hampshire SO45 1AZ. Specimen and transparency in Herb. Hort. Wisley.

First Class Certificate

Rhododendron **'Bach Choir'** (*R. fortunei* × Jalisco Group). First Class Certificate, 19 May 1997, as a hardy flowering plant for exhibition. Trusses of *c.* 8 flowers, loose, to 180mm across. Corolla funnel-campanulate to 70mm long and 90mm across, 7 slightly retuse lobes. Corolla pinkish red (51B) in bud; throat and mouth yellow-orange (19A), deepening to pinkish red (48C) on lobes, outside of corolla pinkish red (48C) and yellow streaked. Stamens 14, held within; filaments white; anthers pale brown. Style and stigma green; style glandular towards base; ovary glandular. Calyx irregularly 6-7 lobed, to 15mm, pale yellowish orange (18B). Leaves oblong to oblanceolate, 110 × 40mm, hairless, matt green above, slightly glaucous beneath; petioles green. Crossed and raised by Fred Wynniatt. Exhibited by Mr E de Rothschild, Exbury Gardens, Exbury, Hampshire SO45 1AZ. Specimen and transparency in Herb. Hort. Wisley.

Corrections to the 1996-97 Year Book

p77 line 20: for 'Sensation' read 'Scentsation'
p78 line 23: for 10mm read 50mm.

Book Reviews

The Encyclopedia of Rhododendron Species by **Peter A Cox & Kenneth N E Cox. 396pp, 1997, Glendoick Publishing UK £75 + £4.50 p & p (see below)**
It can be nothing but good news when rhododendron enthusiasts are notified of a new book by the Cox family, in this case father Peter and son Kenneth and more so in view of the quality of this publication.

The stated aim of the book is to provide a fully comprehensive, well illustrated volume describing all temperate species of rhododendron in cultivation and which could act as a help to identification of each species and, indeed, the species described certainly meet the target.

A full discussion of taxonomy is followed by one on identification of species and an explanation of the hardiness figures given based on experience at the family nursery at Glendoick in Scotland. Two maps give outline details of the provinces of China and the Sino-Himalayan region. Details of the format used give an explanation of the botanical description, distribution in the wild, differences from near relatives, cultural information with dates of introduction and flowering periods in the UK. The descriptive text for each species is backed up by some 1,500 mostly excellent colour photographs, many taken in the wild by the authors.

This is a first class publication by two men who have not only collected in the wild but have had long experience of growing rhododendrons in their own nursery and it must certainly feature in the library of any rhododendron species enthusiast and of any botanical learning institution. The coverage is almost fully up to date but it must be appreciated that rhododendron taxonomy is in a state of constant flux as is, indeed, stated in the text and by reference to the Addendum where the differences between the present book and the RHS publication *Rhododendron Handbook –Species in Cultivation* published at the end of 1997, are noted.

Available in the UK only from the publishers at Glendoick Publishing, Glendoick Gardens Ltd, Glencarse, Perth, PH2 7NS, Scotland.
Post and packing overseas (except USA) £8.
Residents of USA should apply to Rhododendron Species Foundation, PO Box 3798, Federal Way, WA 98063-3798.

BRUCE ARCHIBOLD

The Rothschild Gardens by **Miriam Rothschild, Kate Garton & Lionel Rothschild. (Photos, Andrew Lawson & L. de Rothschild). 190pp, 1996, Gaia Books, £25.**
The Rhododendron fraternity is familiar with the name of Rothschild and constantly acknowledges its debt to Lionel de Rothschild and his garden at Exbury, but not all of us were aware of how many other gardens, in Britain and elsewhere, have been created by members of the family. Miriam Rothschild has now given us a book, superbly illustrated, that tells us the story of how

RHS Rhododendron, Camellia and Magnolia Group

List of Officers and Members of the Committee 1997

Chairman Mr John BOND, LVO, VMH, Georgia Lodge, Buckhurst Road, Cheapside, Ascot, Berkshire SL5 7RP (Tel: 01344 25084)

Vice-Chairman Mr G Alan HARDY, VMH, Hillhurst Farm, Hythe, Kent CT21 4HU (Tel: 01303 266516)

Hon. Treasurer Mr Alastair T STEVENSON, 24 Bolton Road, Grove Park, London W4 3TB (Tel: 0181 994 0584)

Hon. Secretary Mrs Josephine M WARREN, Netherton, Buckland Monachorum, Yelverton, Devon PL20 7NL (Tel: 01822 854022)

Hon. Membership Secretary Mr C A WESTON, Whitehills, Newton Stewart, Scotland DG8 6SL (Tel: 01671 402049 Fax 01671 403106)

Hon. Tours Organizer Mrs Valerie ARCHIBOLD, Starveacre, Dalwood, E Devon EX13 7HH (Tel: 01404 881221)

Hon. Year Book Editor Mr Philip D Evans, Painswold, Broad Street, Cuckfield, W Sussex RH17 5LL (Tel: 01444 450788)

Hon. Bulletin Editor Mrs Eileen WHEELER, Llwyngoras, Crymych, Pembrokeshire SA41 3XW (Tel: 01239 820464)

Committee Members

Mr David FARNES, 5 Pine View, off Deerlands Road, Ashgate, Chesterfield, Derbyshire S40 4DN (Tel: 01246 272105)

Dr R H L JACK, Edgemoor, Loch Road, Lanark ML11 9BG (Tel: 01555 663021)

Miss Cicely PERRING, 47 Havelock Road, Hastings, Sussex TN34 1BQ (Tel: 01424 437081)

Major T Le M SPRING SMYTH, 1 Elcombe's Close, Lyndhurst, Hants SO43 7DS (Tel: 01703 282478)

Mr Ivor STOKES, Pantcoch, Carmel, Llanelli, Dyfed SA14 7SG (Tel: 01269 844048)

Branch Organizers

International Mr Michael JURGENS, The Old House, Silchester, Reading, Berkshire
    RG7 2LU (Tel: 01734 700240)

N Ireland Mr Patrick FORDE, Seaforde, Downpatrick, Co Down BT30 8PG
    (Tel: 01396 811225, Fax: 01396 811370)

S Ireland Mr F W VOGEL, Kells House, Kells Bay, Co Kerry, Eire (Tel: 00 353 667 7605)

Lakeland Mr Peter HOWARTH, 2 Wanlass Howe Flats, Borrans Road, Ambleside, Cumbria
    LA22 0EN (Tel: 01539 432807)

New Forest Mr Christopher FAIRWEATHER, The Garden Centre, High Street, Beaulieu,
    Hants SO42 7YR (Tel: 01590 612307, Fax: 01590 612519)

Norfolk Mrs J M IDIENS, Beaconswood, Roman Camp, Sandy Lane, West Runton,
    Cromer, Norfolk NR27 9ND (Tel: 01263 837779)

North Wales and Northwest Mr J Ken HULME, Treshnish, 72 Parkgate Road, Neston,
    S Wirral L64 6QQ (Tel: 0151 336 8852)

Peak District Mr David FARNES, 5 Pine View off Deerlands Road Ashgate, Chesterfield,
    Derbyshire, S40 4DN (Tel: 01246 272105)

Scottish Mrs Tessa KNOTT, Glenwhan, Dunragit-by-Stranraer DG9 8PH
    (Tel: 01581 400222)

Southeast Mr John E HILLIARD, 99 Gales Drive, Three Bridges, Crawley, Sussex
    RH10 1QD (Tel: 01293 522859)

Southwest Dr Alun J B EDWARDS, 12 Ellerslie Road, Barnstaple, Devon, EX31 2HT
    (Tel: 01271 43324)

Southwest Wales Mr Ivor STOKES, Pantcoch, Carmel, Llanelli, Dyfed SA14 7SG
    (Tel: 01269 844048)

Wessex Mrs Miranda GUNN, Ramster, Petworth Road, Chiddingfold, Surrey GU8 4SN
    (Tel: 01428 644422)

INDEX

DUNGE VALLEY GARDENS
& HARDY PLANT NURSERY

A BEAUTIFUL 6 ACRE RHODODENDRON GARDEN
& HARDY PLANT NURSERY IN THE PEAK NATIONAL PARK

We have one of the best selections of species and hybrid
Rhododendrons for sale in this part of the country including
many large leaved species such as:
R. falconeri, R. fictolacteum, R. hodgsonii,
R. kasangiae, R. siderium, R. sinogrande
and other species including *R. bureavii, R. campylocarpum,*
R. elegantulum, R. flinkii, R. fulgens, R. hunnewellianum,
R. pachysanthum R. roxieanum oreonastes, R. setosum.
Our large range of hybrids include R. Polar Bear, R. Loderi King
George, with many of the new yellows such as R. Hotei,
R. Nancy Evans, and R. Top Banana. Also an extensive
range of unusual trees, shrubs and perennials.
We have larger Hybrid Rhododendrons for sale
in 15, 25 & 45 litre pots to order only.
A5 S.A.E. for catalogue.

The Gardens are open every
day 10-30am. to 6-00pm.
1st April to 31st August
Entry fee £2.50 weekdays
£3.00 Sat, Sun & Bank Hols.
Children 50p. No dogs please.
Other times nursery open
by appointment only.
No mail order
Season Tickets only £4.50 each
Tea Room for light refreshments
Coaches and groups
by appointment only

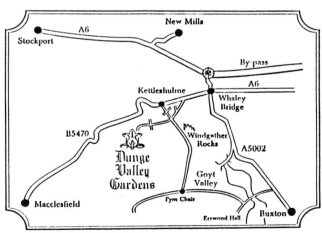

Dunge Valley Gardens & Hardy Plant Nursery, Windgather Rocks,
Kettleshulme, Nr. Whaley Bridge, High Peak, Cheshire, SK23 7RF.
Tel / Fax: 01663 733787.

SLOCOCK & KNAP HILL NURSERIES

RHODODENDRONS & AZALEAS

-

GROWERS FOR GENERATIONS

-

**28 GOLD MEDALS AT THE
CHELSEA FLOWER SHOW
AND A GOLD MEDAL AT THE
1997 RHODODENDRON SHOW**

Our catalogue/price list

is available by post from

KNAP HILL NURSERY LTD.

Send 3 x 1st class stamps

Personal callers welcome by appointment.

SLOCOCK & KNAP HILL NURSERIES
Barrs Lane, Knaphill, Woking, Surrey GU21 2JW
Tel. 01483 481214 FAX 01483 797261
NURSERY OPEN 9am – 5pm MONDAY/FRIDAY
But CLOSED at weekends and Bank Holidays

LWL NURSERIES

Growers of Fine Plants

Specialist growers of :

- Rhododendron hybrids - dwarf to tall
- Rhododendron species
- Yakushimanum hybrids
- Deciduous azaleas
- Evergreen azaleas
- Camellias
- Pieris

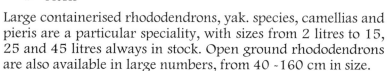

Large containerised rhododendrons, yak. species, camellias and pieris are a particular speciality, with sizes from 2 litres to 15, 25 and 45 litres always in stock. Open ground rhododendrons are also available in large numbers, from 40 -160 cm in size.

SPRING '98 Ten acres of woodland and grassland gardens with mature rhododendrons and azaleas, open for viewing during the flowering season. Please telephone for details.

Delivery and planting services are available, in conjunction with a planting plan design service, to ensure that existing plants and new purchases can be combined in harmony.

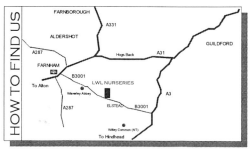

HOW TO FIND US

Opening Hours

Monday - Friday
9.00am- 5.00pm

Saturday & Sunday
10.00am- 4.00pm

Charles Hill, B3001, Tilford, Farnham, Surrey, GU10 2AT
Tel: 01252 703375   Fax: 01252 702858
WebPage : www.LWL.co.uk   Email   : plants@lwl.co.uk

EXBURY GARDENS & PLANT CENTRE

With a tradition for quality breeding of rare and beautiful plants, Exbury Plant Centre – adjacent to Exbury Gardens – offers a wide selection of home-grown rhododendrons, azaleas and camellias.

- Individual enquiries welcome
- Expert advice always available
- Many mature examples to be seen in Exbury's famous 200-acre woodland garden

OPEN DAILY 10am - 5.30pm (OR DUSK).
March to October.

Catalogue available from: The Estate Office, Exbury, Southampton SO45 1AZ. Telephone 01703 891203

ON THE EDGE OF THE NEW FOREST, NEAR BEAULIEU

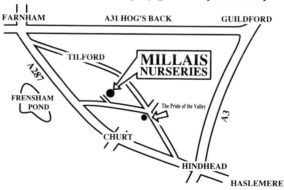